GET LUCKY and STAY LUCKY

GET LUCKY and STAY LUCKY

A Collection of Short Stories

Daryl Riersgard

ISBN-13: 978-1-7351215-0-5
Cover Design: Margarita Felix
Editor: Amy Pattee Colvin

Dedication

This book is dedicated to my father, Ray Riersgard. He was a major influence on my life and offered plenty of father-son mentoring in the early years, including being the volunteer coach of the small grade school basketball team and an even larger effort as the volunteer scoutmaster for my troop and me.

Both efforts required valuable time away from his farming. He was kind and loving to me. He knew how to show affection. He was kind to all those around him. He loved to laugh, and he was fond of his own jokes. He supported my efforts as a farm boy trying to compete in local sports.

As I grew older, he served as a good listener as I projected my goals, especially in my military career. I will always regret that while I was a young and reckless 21-year-old helo pilot in Vietnam, he was home wondering if I would come back alive. When the CBS evening news reported Marine casualties in the helicopter community, he would pull up a chair and wait on the front porch for the black sedan with the Navy Chaplain to arrive. Those had to be painful hours.

Fortunately, the sedan never arrived, and I survived with some major battle scars that eventually healed. I also regret that he died too young to meet my children. I know he would have been proud of the three grandchildren that showed up after the cancer took him.

Contents

Introduction

Better late than never is an old phrase, often used. In my case, the phrase fits my dream of being a competent writer. In 1968 I graduated from Minot State College as an English Major. Soon after, I entered the Marine Corps and became part of the normal squadron environment. In addition to flying, we pilots all had secondary assignments in such areas as Admin, Intelligence, Operations, Logistics, Maintenance or perhaps, NATOPS Officer, Safety Officer, and so on.

Because of my English major background, I was forever cast in the role of the Admin Guy. This meant that I was in charge of all paperwork, pay matters, etc. And, as my military career progressed, it was a role that I could not shake. At one point, I was selected to be the speechwriter for General Homer Hill at the 3rd Marine Air Wing. I had no experience speechwriting, but I managed to fumble my way through that job. Later, I was the Personnel Officer for an Air Group.

Eventually, my admin experience culminated in a role as a Pentagon staff officer. In that role, I served as a readiness analyst, but each February, I was responsible for drafting the Congressional Testimony in support of the annual budget hearings. These formal hearings included both the HASC and SASC, House Armed Services Committee and Senate Armed Services Committee.

This role was both challenging and fun and took months of preparation before my General presented the testimony that I had drafted. Essentially, through most of my Marine Corps years, I wrote actively. However, most of the writing was technical rather than creative.

In 2005, the year I bought a small ranch in Paradise Valley, I did attempt to write creatively. During the less busy winter months, I drafted a non-fiction book called *Martin Creek*, an account of my first year on the ranch, patterned after the book *Walden Pond*. After finishing my manuscript, I decided not to publish it, so it sits somewhere as an unfinished work.

Even if I did not consider myself as a novel writer, I did consider myself a raconteur. I have always felt comfortable relating a good story or a long-standing joke. I believe I have a long personal library of such stories, and I enjoy sharing them.

The topic of creative writing remained silent until 2019 when I traveled to Washington D.C. to attend the interment ceremony of General Roscoe Combs at Arlington Cemetery. Ten of us assembled from across the country to pay our respects to an old Vietnam squadron mate. We were all combat buddies with a special bond.

By design, the group met a couple of days prior to the Interment, and thus we had another mini-reunion. Gatherings similar to this happened many times over the past 50 years.

These meetings are characterized by the old days of drinking beer or scotch, and telling war stories. Some stories get retold over and over again. Some stories need to be pried out of the storyteller. When it was my turn, I recounted the day that I got shot down in Vietnam, 27 October 1970. Some events do not fade over time because the memories are so vivid, and some stories get refined with repeated telling.

After I shared my story, a number of my squadron mates were surprised because they had not heard this tale before. At the conclusion, there was friendly arm twisting for me to write a book. I knew that this was not a realistic possibility; however, I was willing to consider a collection of short stories. Many of these stories had already been put to paper for the sake of my children.

Most writers seem to have a role model or favorite author that they can pattern their work after. One of my favorite authors has been Barry Lopez. I have read his work from *Winter Count* to *Crossing Open Ground* to the more recent *Horizons*.

I decided to pattern my work after his collection of short stories, told in *Winter Count*. This book includes over a dozen short stories with over a hundred pages. While I will never achieve his vocabulary, I do like his approach to sharing a story. He produces both fiction and non-fiction stories and books. My book is 100% non-fiction.

On the other hand, there is Karl Ove Knausgaard, the Norwegian writer who searched for a style he could copy. Finally, out of frustration, Karl decided to abandon any other style and just to start to write. I have only read his first book, *My Struggle*, but I am good with his approach of no particular style of writing.

Ernest Hemingway once said that writing is easy. You just sit down to a typewriter and start to bleed.

This collection starts with a horrific day in Vietnam when I got shot down and narrowly escaped with my life. I also share another scary event when I was involved in a mid-air crash over the Pacific at night. This was also survived, but it probably aged me many years in one terrifying hour. Near the end of my collection is a peaceful account of life on a remote ranch.

Since my life had more to offer than just scary helo events, I shared stories from other parts of my long life. I spent 20 years in Marine aviation, 16 years in law enforcement, and 14 years operating a small ranch in remote Northern Nevada. All too often, my stories of adventure and survival reflect *a pattern of being lucky*, which explains, in part, why I'm still around at this ripe old age.

© Thomas C. Smith

Recover crew salvaging radios and other reusable parts from the crash site a day or so later.

Vietnam Crash and Burn

This story recounts my catastrophic helicopter crash on 27 October 1970, from the moments before the crash to the half-hour after the crash.

As a backdrop to this story, the United States was weighing a painful decision about reinstating the draft system. The Vietnam war pressed on much longer than anticipated. Consequently, the military, especially the U.S. Army, was having trouble filling its ranks.

As a result, the national draft started on 1 December 1969. A system was used to put capsules into a hopper and have someone pull them out in the order of draft call ups. The first number on the draft calendar was 14 December, and the last call-up date was 8 June. Later, it was determined that more names were called-up on one part of the year versus the other half of the year. Someone determined that this was a result of the way the capsules were dumped into the hopper. So, 195 names were called-up, and 170 names were draft-free.

I never learned what my birth date was on this pecking order. By 1970 it did not matter.

Furthermore, I was a volunteer, like the rest of the Marines. I knew the draft system was coming, so I signed up for the Marine Officer Candidate Program years prior. Consequently, this game of drawing dates from a hopper had no bearing on me. I was already heading for the war, draft, or no draft.

Background

The aircraft involved was bureau number 154838. The crew had been assigned night medevac the night before. The crew consisted of aircraft commander Lt. Gary Denton, copilot, Lt. Daryl Riersgard, and the crew chief was Cpl Gary Radliff. Fortunately, our medevac crew had little activity that night and were reasonably well-rested.

After we were relieved, the flight operations went into the day time routine. Another aircraft was assigned to a medevac mission, and it was forced down due to enemy fire. That crew was uninjured. However, the flight operations staff needed to replace that medevac mission with a new crew.

Our crew, still assembled and just finishing breakfast, was asked to take over the mission. I had been told that it was bad luck to volunteer for a mission after another crew had been forced down. Perhaps that perception is true. Our entire crew volunteered anyway.

Our morning started out routinely. We were doing medevacs and had just picked up four or five, none of which were of a emergency nature. We continued to pick up injured Marines throughout the morning.

The next pick up was assigned to Hill 270 South, a mountain top none of the crews cared for because it was a tiny landing zone. If you were good or lucky, you could get the three-landing gears onto the ground. Many pilots struggled with this landing zone.

At this point in my combat experience, I was oper-ating with incautious bravado. Nothing could possibly go wrong because I was a Marine pilot, and my skills exceed any danger. Ya right!

Accident Details

As the pilot approached the zone, it appeared to me that we were way too high for a normal approach and landing. Because the approach was higher than normal, the pilot attempted to reduce power and back into the landing zone. Since we were not over level ground, it was hard to assess our actual altitude. I would guess we were between 200' and 300' above the zone, 30 stories up.

In order to recover from a bad approach, the pilot hovered for a long time, trying to get back over the zone. This meant that he backed up, and the nose of the helicopter was higher than normal. This also meant that we made ourselves a wonderful target for the enemy. After realizing that the pilot was struggling, I made the impromptu decision to push the stick forward

3

because this approach was getting very uncomfortable. Also, at that moment, I realized that we were under enemy fire.

The next sensation was a loud explosion in the back of the aircraft. Concurrent with this noise was a loud shudder, and I saw a rotor blade fly by the left side of the aircraft. My first thought was that it looked like a boomerang flying into the distance. Now it was clear that we were in grave danger. My thought at the time was, "this is going to hurt a lot," for we were quite a distance above the top of the landing zone.

As soon as the rotor system intermeshed, we went from being an airworthy aircraft to a 26,000-pound rock, or in this case, a shattered hunk of metal.

We were surrounded by a cacophony of noise as the aircraft broke apart and made impact twice. From the moment of intermesh until we finally crashed into the rock pile, we were surrounded by clamor and violent movement.

I embodied a sense of wild panic. This whole phase was probably less than half a minute, but the impact on my brain and my sense of survival instinct will be everlasting. I felt bad for the Marines in the back of the helo because most were not strapped in. Possibly the crew chief was on a safety strap, but the gunners and the medevac victims were no doubt bouncing around the cabin area like dice rattled in a cup. Somehow, everyone stayed inside the wreckage, likely due to death grips onto something solid.

A study of the wreckage and wreckage photos show an explosion splintered and burned the right stub wing. The two stub wings also served as the fuel tanks, and one entire stub wing was missing, and the burn damage showed alongside the fuselage.

At the point when I pushed the nose forward, the helicopter had assumed a sort of nose down, ski jump attitude to the slope of the mountain. In my estimation, the only way we could have survived a 200' to 300' fall was for the aircraft to be in a favorable pitch, nose down to match the angle of the mountainside.

Because I was knocked unconscious with the impact, I don't remember the details of hitting the ground. As I realized later, I was knocked unconscious thanks to my heavy bullet bouncer, which was strapped into my seat harness. Upon impact, my head was likely snapped forward as my knees pushed the bullet bouncer into my chin. Later, it was clear that I had a patch of skin missing from my chin, so this supported my theory.

The impact was so violent that the back one-third portion of the helo broke away from the rest of the aircraft. The breakpoint was at the vulnerable 410 section next to the ramp. The section that broke away included the rear rotor system, which came to rest probably less than 100-yards from the top of the landing zone. When the dust settled, the front part of the helo was about 80 yards from the aft.

I was unconscious only briefly as I recall the wild roller coaster ride down the side of this steep mountain. This ride seemed to last an eternity, but probably only covered a few hundred yards down the South-East slope of the mountain. The wreckage not only bounced across rough terrain but rolled from side to side on the way down.

The tumultuous ride lasted until the remaining section of the helo crashed into a house-sized pile of rocks. I was awake during this turbulent event, and awake as the front of the helo slammed into the rockpile—the sketch at the beginning of this story depicts this scene—and then I lost consciousness again.

I have no way of knowing how long I was out, but when I awoke, I realized the wreckage was on fire. As I looked around, I realized that the upper portion of the cockpit had been crushed to the inside. The top illustration depicts the rock pile that the wreckage finally crashed into. Had we not stopped here, it's possible that we would have continued to the base of the mountain where the enemy gunfire had come from.

When I looked over to the pilot, he was not moving, and there was red fluid covering his upper torso. He appeared to be dead. My first thought was that the red fluid must be blood; however, later, I realized it was hot hydraulic fluid, which has a red color, that came from a cracked forward transmission located over the heads of both pilots.

At this point, the fight for survival kicks in, and your body and brain are in a wild rush to get to someplace safer. Since I could see fire in the area of the crew's door, I decided to escape through the side emergency hatch. When I pulled the emergency release lever, the door fell away from the cockpit because the helo was now laying on its port, left, side.

I unhooked my lap belt and shoulder straps, rolled out of the cockpit, and fell about six feet. Because the rock pile partially supported us, there was room between the cockpit and the ground. In the panic of the moment, I forgot to undo the plug to my helmet. As a result, when I rolled out of the cockpit, my neck snapped as the plug undid itself. At this point, I felt exceedingly disoriented.

After leaving the aircraft, I found myself inside a pocket where the wreckage was above me, and the rocks were in front of me. My instinct was to get around the pilot's side of the wreckage. By this time, the Corpsman and crew chief were helping recover the rest of the crew. As we worked on getting the unconscious pilot out, I saw the rest of the crew and the medevaced Marines slowly stumbling out the crew's door located on the right side, or now the top side, of the wreckage.

In order to extricate the pilot, someone had to crawl back into the cockpit to release his emergency hatch. When we unhooked him from his straps, we had a difficult time lifting him out. The seat was in an awkward position, and the pilot weighed more than any of the other crew members. Three of us pulled on the pilot, trying to get him out of the seat. It was only near the end of the extrication that the pilot started to regain consciousness.

Throughout this recovery process, we realized we were in a crossfire between the Marines on the top of the zone and enemy fire closer to the bottom of the mountain. We assumed that the enemy fire was the same enemy fire that took down our aircraft.

It was a long crawl and struggle up the side of the mountain. The ground was wet and slippery. The terrain was steep. Injured and in shock, we grappled with the hillside, helping one another progress toward the top. The Marines above paused their firefight long enough to help us reach safety at the top of the landing zone.

Post Script

It is unusual for a co-pilot to take the controls from the pilot. I have no way of knowing if the pilot recognized that I had pushed the stick forward while he was trying to back up the helo. I thought he would address this point after the crash, but he did not. I thought he might address this matter at a subsequent reunion, but, unfortunately, the pilot was killed in another crash after Vietnam.

Many years later, during a Pop-a Smoke reunion, a large poster-size photo of the crash was awarded to T.C. Davis, since he also survived a crash. When T.C. saw the image, he commented that this was not his crash. He said, and others confirmed that it looked like the Riersgard crash, so the poster mounted on hardback was handed over to me. That poster rests in a safe place in my office.

Immediately after the accident, I realized that I had suffered a bullet wound through my left shin. The round entered the calf, hit the shin bone, and then glanced to the side. The wound hole was between 1" and 2" deep. It took nearly six weeks for that wound to heal so that I could return to flight status. The wound turned purple and green as gangrene set in.

I learned later I had also broken my lower back with seven vertebrae crushed. I suffered for years from back problems after the crash. Eventually, those back issues improved.

My leg wound eventually healed from the inside out. It took almost two months before that hole started to look normal. Today, it is nothing but another scar on a beat-up old body. At the time, all my friends and roommates would run away when it was time for me to take a chopstick and push the clean gauze into the wound. This would normally be a 3-foot long strip that I packed into the wound. Inserting the clean gauze was the nice part of the process. Pulling out the wet and colorful old gauze was not so nice. But time heals all wounds.

Many of us suffered minor burns wherever skin was exposed, for example, on necks and arms, if the flight suit was rolled up. Not all of us survived crashes or other war battles.

This story may be the *best example of not good luck, but great luck.* By most accounts, everyone onboard that helo should have died on that date in October 1970.

On this topic of luck, two statistics cause me pain. First, 997, which is the number of folks in Vietnam who were killed during their first day. Second, 1448, which is the number of people killed during their last day. Most of the pilots that I knew had a lingering fear that their last flight could literally be their last flight.

For perspective, this is what the helicopter looked like before the crash.

Finding My Remote Ranch

It is often said that going full circle is part of the life process. In other words, yes, you can return home. In my case, I started on a farm/ranch, then spent a full life and career in the military, then somehow returned to a ranch to complete my full circle.

It is also said that people who are happy have a sense of appreciation. I can say with full certainty that I am happy at this stage of life—age 68 when I wrote this chapter—possibly because I appreciate what this ranch property brings me. In short, it is the simple sublimity of the ranch surroundings. For example, I appreciate the green meadow south of the ranch house, the high rock canyon where Martin Creek comes out of the mountains to the east, the snow-capped Santa Rosa Mountains to the north, or the valley view to the west. Sure, other things that bring value, but this story is about the ranch and the advantages it brings.

As I begin this chapter, I acknowledge that ranch life has presented me with meaningful work. Most men find some satisfaction in working hard; however, we always look for something more. This ranch has offered both: meaningful work and something more. The something more includes those subtle qualities of life features that come with your surroundings. I have often acknowledged the sheer beauty of the ranch surrounding. While these surroundings are important, it is also important to share this setting with my family. They may not visit the ranch often, but when they do come, we have good experiences. Work stops, and the play begins. We travel the canyons, the hills, and the mountains. We explore. When the day is done, we find solace and comfort in each other's company. We enjoy the meals that I prepare. I often receive help from the adult kids. Simple pleasures combine to create a good life.

I have often pondered the questions of how did I get here, how did this ranch find me, or how did I get so lucky? I can say that it was my intent all along to find a rural property after my working days were over. Before I found this particular ranch, I was open-minded. I looked far and wide for the best location. I even considered rebuilding Grandpa's homestead back to its former state. I looked seriously at many other locations in Nevada. Most of these spots were quiet and remote. I sometimes took friends along so I could get another perspective as to whether a given site was for me. These searches continued until I found this place in Paradise Valley.

I was introduced to this general location during a trip to the Gastanaga property, thanks to Chris, a cousin through marriage. This is a 1000-acre island parcel of beauty set back into the national forest. Cottonwood Creek runs through it. Aspens flourish and cover the hills where beautiful quad trails weave, up and down. The site is so special that the USFS often tries to buy it back. The family, long consistent in their answer, always replies, "No, thanks."

Following that extended weekend trip in May, I started a search in the surrounding valley—Paradise Valley. Eddie was my real estate agent and guide. Eddie showed me everything from 800-acre ranches to many smaller undeveloped sites in the 15-18-acre range. I should say that while I was energized in this pursuit, I should admit that I did follow one basic rule, and that was that the final location should be within commuting distance to Reno, in this case, three-and-one-half hours away.

I quickly focused my attention on the 17.5-acre site owned by Dan and Kelly, up for sale because of their recent divorce. I may have taken too much time to think about this decision because later, I saw the property listed in a glossy real estate magazine out of Reno. When the magazine hit the streets, Eddie informed me that five people were in line, ready to look at it. This was all the incentive I needed to make a commitment in 2005 to buy it.

I liked this site because it was at the far end of the valley and invited little traffic. I also appreciated the assortment of scenery. I share this observation twice because the ranch setting is so special. If you take a perspective at the top step of the property, you see Muffler Meadow to the south. This is a vast green meadow that supports summer-long cattle grazing on the Old Mill Ranch. The other nice feature is that this meadow is home to a large flock of wild Rio turkeys. If you move your scan to the east, you are looking up Martin Creek canyon. This is a high rock canyon, carved out by Martin Creek. The backdrop here is the geographic feature called Sugarloaf.

Another rarely seen feature up the high rock canyon is the mountain lions living in the caves. Looking north and east, you see the Red Hills. This is a high rock feature serving as a transition to the Santa Rosa Mountains. Finally, if you look to the north, you can see the Santa Rosa Mountains. At the time of this writing, late March, the mountains are snow-capped.

A long time ago, someone told me that if you can't afford to buy a large tract of land, then buy land next to a national forest. In my case, I only have a bit more than 17 acres, but I have 330,000-acres of public land managed by the USFS out the back gate. Maybe I should say that it is partially managed by the government, but that will be saved for another story.

I had another reason to make this move. A few years prior, I was in a head-on car accident with a drunken teenage driver. It was like a scene right out of Fast and Furious. My settlement from that accident was approximately the same figure as the sales price on the property. Was this serendipity? This made the ranch purchase an easy choice.

This was mostly an undeveloped property, but it was fenced, had a well, and had power pulled. Oh yes, and it had a nice circular driveway.

I made the determination a long time ago that if you are going to build a house, it is wise to build a shop first. This is even truer if you have a tool collection that would otherwise be outside in the weather.

Consequently, the 40' x 50' shop was constructed in 2006. This was good for me because the structure was large enough to handle my motor home. It was my intent to live in the motor home while I watched my ranch house being built.

The ranch house was constructed later in 2006/2007. Many years later, a bunkhouse was added next to the main house. This is the topic of a separate story.

This account reflects having a purpose in life. Every morning when I got up, I had a long list of projects. When first entering the property, you'll see massive amounts of rock borders. The property came with an oversupply of rocks, so I had a choice to haul them off or find a place for each one.

When I started to analyze my hours of rock movement, I made the decision that no one gets to sell this ranch. I have invested too much to have someone else sell the property and run off with the profit. However, sometimes life doesn't go as planned.

Most of my planning was sound, and with one exception, I did not change the development sequence. The exception was the addition of my 33 hp John Deere tractor. By the time I purchased the tractor, I already dug scores of post holes by hand. I'd moved hundreds of immense rocks, rocks truly too big for my damaged back. I was three or four years into the ranch development before I bought the tractor. I should have done this on the first day.

A difficult post hole can take half a day to dig by hand compared to a minute with the tractor posthole digger. For an older man, this addition was crucial.

Years ago, I heard a radio interview with one of my favorite people, Wendell Berry. He is a poet and author who owns a small farm in Arkansas. He was asked how much farm work was involved. He answered by saying that the farm was a full-time concern but not a full- time job. That is kind of true here unless I am on a roll with major projects, in which case it is a full-time job.

Okay, so where is the quality of life in all of this.

While lots of ranch progress has been realized over the past fourteen years, it is only fair to report that there has been a steady dose of pleasure at the same time. One prime example of ranch pleasure came from the decision to raise a rare breed of Sheep from St. Kilda Island. St. Kilda is west of Scotland. The breed is known as Soay. This scene is depicted in the sketch at the top of this story.

I always start my morning with a brief prayer of thanks. That prayer is for the opportunity to enjoy another day of ranch life. The great unknown is how many more of these days are left in the larger game plan. Since that answer is unknown, my role is to enjoy the days while they last.

The ranch mornings always start slowly with plenty of coffee. When the season is right, that coffee is enjoyed on the sunny side of the porch. The sunny side of the porch is also the side of the main garden. When the season is right, I enjoy fresh raspberries and peaches with my coffee. When the fruit is in short supply, I simply walk the garden or even move a chair to a favorite spot and soak up the bucolic atmosphere of the garden and the view.

While writing this, in late March, I took a brief break and walked the front yard with coffee in hand. The spring has been warm, and the trees are confused. They don't know if it is safe to bud and bloom or if they should hold back. The only trees with leaf development are the crab apples. The daffodils are in early bloom. The Persian lilacs are starting to show some green. Down in the orchard, the apricot tree is in full bloom and is usually the first casualty of the "false spring" where a hard freeze destroys the fruit crop before it gets a chance to start the growth process.

Wind is a reality of living at the mouth of a canyon. When the summer gets hot, this breeze is a blessing. This blessing is never more important than during the two hottest months of late summer. When the temperature rises and creates midday heat, the breeze flows up the canyon. When the temperature cools in the evening and early morning hours, the breeze reverses course and comes down canyon. During cooler seasons, the morning breeze tends to keep me indoors, and this is when I read my morning papers, catch up on paperwork, and maybe do some short story writing.

Thomas Jefferson described his daily routine as "arts and letters" in the morning and garden work in the afternoon. In my case, I pay bills in the early morning and then go back to hard labor.

Generally, by mid-morning, it is time to get headed to some serious ranch work.

Ranch work is another quality of life example. When the day is done, and a cold beer is in hand, I can look back at what was accomplished today. There is a good feeling associated with the mental video replay, where I look back at what I achieved.

Late afternoons are when I start to wind down. I will sometimes take a bottle of wine and visit a special spot. This spot is alongside a canal running midway through my property. The spot is surrounded by honey locust trees. Because this flat spot has a beach-like feature, it soon developed the name, Beach Corral. I sit in the easy chair, watch my animals, and get a wine buzz on—another quality of life indicator.

In December 2011, I got sick and had to rely on afternoon naps as part of my physical recovery. This was the first time in my life that I had an excuse for a one-hour nap. As I found out later, Winston Churchill was dedicated to his daily naps. Now years later, I still find time to repeat this routine. Being well-rested is a good thing for an older body.

The days are not always spent doing ranch chores. Before I got involved in weed control work, I used to grab a six-pack and a book, jump on the quad and drive up canyon past the fishpond. I would drive the quad into shallow Martin Creek and would stop at shady parts of the stream. I would read and drink until I could not focus.

It is unknown what kind of family interest there will be in the ranch after I am gone. Christian has shown keen interest in the short term. If this happens, the property may need to be split into three separate lots with houses on each.

When that day comes, this ranch development will be pretty much complete. This was my thought process up until April 2019 when I made the difficult decision to sell.

Again, *finding this beautiful location had to be a stroke of luck.* There were bigger ranches, but none had the same unbelievable views sitting on top of that west bank ledge. While San Antonio is a perfect fit, I will forever miss those ranch views and the associated ranch memories. Red Bud, the Soay ram pictured next page, is a classic example of a fond ranch memory. He sired many healthy lambs.

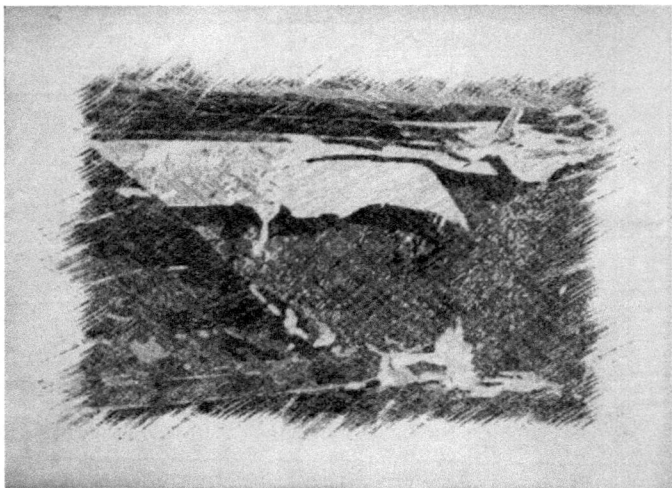

Mid-air Crash Over the Pacific

I have a coffee cup with the date of 17 December 1978 written on the side. That was the date of my mid-air crash, perhaps the scariest event of my life. It was scarier than being shot down because that event ended quickly, whereas the mid-air crash seemed to last forever.

The story starts as the helo carrier was sailing from South Korea back to the Philippines. The squadron had a number of aircraft mechanically down awaiting parts. Someone made the decision to order parts out of the Marine Base in Okinawa, and as the carrier passed by to the east, it was determined that two CH-46's should fly ashore to pick up parts. This mission included the Maintenance Officer, and I was the Division Leader for this flight.

We flew from the carrier to the Marine Base in late afternoon. By the time we were loading up the sun was setting and darkness was starting to set in. As we launched and flew eastward towards the carrier, the sky grew blacker by the minute.

Our task was to find the carrier as it headed south. This step was routine as the flight started with a good Tacan lock, and I knew where we were headed. Around 20 minutes into the flight, my Tacan signal faded. I made a radio call to my wingman as to his Tacan status.

Within seconds after my radio call, we heard a loud bang and the aircraft shuddered as if hit by something. Immediately, my helo went out of control with an extreme one-to-one rotor beat, and radical vibrations shook the entire bird. My first sensation was that the controls were swinging madly, both the collective and the cyclic stick. The cyclic was banging off my knees, and the collective was going up and down. Something disastrous had happened to the control, but I had no idea what was causing the problem.

I quickly tried to communicate with my crew; however, the noise and vibration were so severe that I could not hear anyone. Next, I tried to place a "May Day" call on the emergency frequency. The stick was flying around so extremely I could not tell if I had made a successful call or not.

The crew members and passengers in the back knew exactly what had happened because they were all eyewitnesses. However, we, the pilot and co-pilot, had no clue.

My first thought was that this helo could not possibly survive the wild vibrations. I was certain that the helo would shake apart and intermesh into a catastrophic failure. As my mouth went dry, I was certain that a crash and death were soon to follow. Even though I knew my emergency procedures manual very well, it didn't mention how to deal with this problem.

So, I improvised.

At this point, something was controlling the cockpit controls instead of the other way around. The cyclic was banging off my two knees. I tried to use my legs to control the stick, but that did not work well. What the cyclic stick did do was turn the insides of my legs a black and blue color.

I tried to provide some control to the helo as I turned westward toward the island of Okinawa. Remember, I did not have any navigation aids, so I made a wild guess what direction to fly. I still believed that this aircraft was soon to come apart. I tried to find an airspeed and altitude that might allow us to survive if we fell into the ocean. If we did, no one would find us because we were essentially lost at sea and lost in the pitch-dark night.

My wingman had long since abandoned me to do this flight alone. To this day, I ask myself how a squadron-mate could realize how much damage he caused only to fly away, leaving me with a mess on my hands. Since his damage was minimal, he could have flown on my wing until I found a safe landing. But no, he was long gone.

I did my best to take the helo down to around 30 feet above the water and get the airspeed down to about 30 knots. Later, some older savvy helo pilots said that was the right thing to do. I hoped that if the aircraft shook apart, we might be able to survive the ocean impact.

Because the airspeed was so slow, it took forever to see any sign of land. I have no idea how long I flew before my searchlight found a rocky cliff on the shoreline. I would estimate my flight took at least 30 minutes and perhaps as many as 45 minutes. I hoped for a nice sandy beach where I could do a run on crash landing, but that was not in the cards.

My heart pounded, and my mouth was dry—so dry I could not talk—which didn't really matter because no one could hear me.

As I approached the shore, I noticed high tension power lines running parallel to the beach. My first thought was that if I tried to fly over the top, the addition of power might be the final straw, but I was able to gain altitude and clear the power lines. From that higher altitude, I saw a soccer field with my searchlight.

The soccer field was the first piece of good news in over 45-minutes of terror-filled flight.

As I positioned the helo for a running landing, I saw another helo at the far end of the soccer field. I soon realized that was the wingman who had abandoned me over the dark Pacific.

When the rotors slowed to a stop, the Maintenance Officer jumped from my bird and started to run across the field. He headed for the other pilot who was casually walking our way. Bill greeted the other pilot with a punch in the mouth. That seemed to remove the smile that I initially saw.

About this time, the rotors were coasting to a stop, and I could finally hear what was going on. I yelled to the crew chief, "What happened?"

He said, "Take a look at your aft blades as they come around."

What I saw shocked me. Approximately 4 feet of one blade was missing. The other bird lost around 2 inches off his blade when the two rotor systems struck each other.

As we learned later, from the Boeing factory representative, no CH-46 had ever lost that much blade and lived to tell about it. The sketch at the top of this story depicts the extent of the blade damage.

Radio communication was established, and spare blades were flown in from MCAF Futenma. When the blades were swapped, and a thorough inspection was made, my bird was given a test flight. I declined the offer to fly this test hop because I had had enough for one day.

As was determined during the subsequent accident investigation, the other pilot was at the controls when I asked him to check his Tacan. This posed two problems. First, he was flying overlapping rotor blades without this being briefed, and second, he did not ask for any crew help regarding the Tacan question. Instead, the pilot looked down at the navigation aide himself. As he looked down, he allowed his helo to drop down and intermesh our two rotor systems. Normally, you would ask the co-pilot to check the navigation aid, especially since he was flying so close together.

This was the longest scare I have ever had in my life. I asked my co-pilot, Craig Arey, what he thought, and he said he thought that I had everything under control. He asked what I thought, and I said that I thought we were going to die.

The technical representatives from the factory indicated that with that much blade damage, we should have intermeshed and crashed into the sea. Once again, *I had luck on my side*.

Growing Old

This may be a difficult topic to report on honestly. None of us like the fact that old age catches up to everyone. Also, it is tough to figure out when old age has finally hit home. Consequently, this story could continue well past its original telling.

Every time I reflect on old age, the theme of a song that touches my heart comes to mind.

The lyrics were written by John Prine, one of the great singer-songwriters of my generation, who died of coronavirus in April 2020.

Prine has a song called "Hello in There." It deals with old people and loneliness. The lyrics go as follows:

> *"You know that old trees just grow stronger*
> *Old rivers just grow wilder every day*
> *Old people just grow lonesome*
> *Waiting for someone to say, "Hello, in there, Hello."*

Later in the song is a related line,

> *"If you are walking down the street sometime*
> *and you see some hollow ancient eyes,*

please don't pass them by and stare
As if you didn't care, say, "Hello in there, Hello."

Growing old may be synonymous with growing lonely, but not necessarily.

In my case, I find that I enjoy a certain amount of solitude. It gives me time to think and ponder what is going on. However, this is not the case when I need to roll out some sheep wire, and I need a strong back or two. At times like these, having someone around is a luxury.

I also thought that you could be lonely when you are not alone, but it must be easier to grow lonely when you are alone.

At the top of this section is one of my favorite illustrations, a sketch of me getting older with my young puppy. Since moving to the ranch, I have evolved through various stages of being alone. Growing old is a broader topic than just potential loneliness. On a ranch, you are never really alone. There are plenty of sheep to care for, and cow dogs galore.

It is difficult to say when you realize you are growing old; I mean, really growing old. My first clue was when my aviator's eyes started to fail me while reading. I was reluctant to get reading glasses because everyone knows reading glasses are proof of getting older.

My hearing has always been a physical disability, so hearing loss may not be a good indicator of aging for me. This damage goes back to too much time on carrier decks, sitting in the cockpit of large helicopters, not to mention sitting in the front row of many loud rock concerts.

In my early 60's I found that I was doing very little running. I switched over to walking or hiking, and do this regularly, though I should admit that I am often a fair-weather walker. If it is cold and windy, I may skip that day.

Is weight a factor? My weight started to creep up from my fighting days (USMC) when I was a trim 165, maybe 170 on a fat day. Today the weight range is between 180 and 195 and very steady. I refuse to change my diet regarding the things that I enjoy—I eat a muffin in the morning, drink whole milk whenever possible, and consume plenty of bread and pasta. I am not sure what weight has to do with growing old except that less activity may be a factor.

I think the first time I felt really old was the same time that I got really sick in December 2011. My body was giving out, and my psyche was not good. All of the kids came to the hospital to show support. Unfortunately, I felt so tired and so sick that I really wanted them to go away so I could get some rest. I knew it was bad form to invite them away, but we didn't find much to talk about, and rest and recovery was honestly my priority concern.

Each time I passed a decade threshold, I'd think to myself, "I should really be old now." That thought process started when I passed 50, but I didn't really feel old. When I passed 60, the thought came up again, but I really didn't feel much different. Maybe it will hit me as I turn 70; I am 68 at the time of this first draft. As I update this story, I can tell you, turning 70 was no different from the earlier decade steps.

So, what are the real aging indicators for me?

When I hike up a hill, I feel the fatigue that I didn't feel years ago.

I acknowledge that I sleep more. I generally sleep from 8:30 until 5:30, so that amounts to 9 hours. Even when I was middle-aged, I needed 8 hours of sleep though I didn't always get it, especially during my time on graveyard shift. I used to dread driving home after a shift because if there was a red light, I was afraid that I would fall asleep at the stoplight.

During the winter or during bad weather, I now look for an excuse to take a nap. I used to feel guilty about napping, but I am getting over that now. In my 70's, naps have become routine.

When I was younger, I was hyperactive and could not sit still for long. I found this to be the case during a 2.5-hour baseball game. Now, I am very content to sit down and watch an entire game. Maybe this has more to do with patience than old age.

The old-age factor that no one wants to talk about is "memory." I think my memory is okay except for the fact that the hard drive in my brain is full. And, for me, is the factor that both my paternal grandmother Thea and Uncle Ken died of Alzheimer's disease. Oddly both lived to be around 90 years of age.

I have long feared that the frequent back pain of my early and mid-years would get worse with old age. The reality has been just the opposite as I have learned to live with the back injuries.

During early April 2014, I was doing difficult chores when I pulled a muscle in my rib cage. That should not have been a big deal except that I made me feel both weak and ill.

It caused me to recall my post-operative experience after thyroid removal. After routine surgery, I was coming too, and my vital signs started to flat line. This set the room into an immediate panic. I believe I was given a needle shot directly into my heart to kick-start me. After extra time in the hospital trying to figure out what went wrong, they found nothing. The doctor concluded that I was just fragile and vulnerable during medical stress situations. Fragile and vulnerable, for me, relate to old age.

When my daughter Lauren learned about my pulled rib muscles, she called. She first asked how I was feeling. She then launched into a strong lecture about controlling my physical activity, so I wouldn't get injured. I had to explain that this made sense except that ranch chores still need to get done even when there is no one here to help me.

With old age, I find gardening to be the perfect activity. It has a purpose, it is not too large in scope, and it provides visual rewards later, highlighting the value of patience.

I should probably update this story when I turn 78 and 88 and compare the indicators.

For now, I am getting older. I enjoy the change. I have little to complain about because my body parts all still work. I don't have any chronic back, hip, or knee problems. I have had no hint of replacement surgery, hip replacement, or any other sort of replacement. My strength and endurance are probably above average. This comparison is driven home when I compare health indicators with an acquaintance in Paradise town.

He and I were the same age, and his heart was 43% functional. He has a large gut. He is often on bottled oxygen. He often walks with the help of a walker. On the other hand, he overeats, smokes, drinks, and never exercises. He has been in and out of the hospital or old folk's home the past year. Compared to this guy, I feel great.

At one point, when this above individual was struggling, I offered to coach him with some walking for health. We could meet each morning, and I would coach him on a slow recovery. I assured him that I would start with easy walks. I said we could slowly work our way up to longer walks. He politely told me, "No, thanks." He died shortly thereafter.

On a positive note, I was subjected to a series of heart tests to determine if chest pains were related to heart disease. The third and final test was the treadmill stress test. I was expected to work my way up to a fast run pace while the doctor, Dr. Raj Hundal, monitored the sensors. This was a difficult test because I had not run recently. At the end of the test, Dr. Hundal said that I had one of the top 10 strongest hearts he had ever monitored. I asked if this was for my age bracket, and he said no, considering hearts of all ages. He concluded by saying that he had two facts to share. First, was the realization that I would eventually die of something. Second, I would not die of a heart problem.

As a second positive factor, I should mention my prior back problems. I broke my lower back with the helicopter crash in 1970. Twenty years ago, I broke my upper back during a DUI head-on car crash. Even in my 20's and 30's I had frequent back attacks where a slipped disc or something related, would put me in bed for a week or two. After I managed to get back on my feet, my posture was hunched over as I tried to get back to normal activity. This whole process was incredibly painful, but I felt that I needed to get off my back and push for a recovery. After each incident, it would often take 6-8 weeks before I was free of pain and walking normally.

This trend happened a couple of times a year. Over time, I learned that the frequency of back attacks was reduced as I learned how to protect my weak back. Now it is infrequent for me to have a back problem. This is a positive because I was fearful that old age would make the back problems worse.

The key thing with old age is to develop the right attitude to make you a mellow and pleasant guy. Starting each day as a Christian gentleman is my primary intention, given the fact that a good attitude will be tested when idiots and jerks enter the picture. My secondary approach is to avoid contact with the negative people and thus control my quality of life factors.

When I ponder the topic of old age, I often seek role models. One such model would be Norman Maclean, the author of *A River Runs Through It*.

MacLean seemed to split his time between a family cabin in Montana and his academic interests in Chicago and the East Coast. His wife Jessie died in 1968. He died 22 years later. I have found some accounts of his lifestyle and his personal philosophy that reflect he seemed comfortable spending his final years alone.

I also found it interesting that he started his writing career in his early 70's. When he wrote, he confined himself to the kitchen table in his cabin, the same table where he had his breakfast. He decided it would not be a good idea to write on his porch because that setting offered too many distractions. He limited his morning writing to around four hours. In the afternoon, he moved to his favorite fishing stream, where he often fished until dark. Both writing and fishing are solitary activities, and that may explain his comfort level of living alone.

I can't help but keep track of my Vietnam buddies. At our last reunion a couple of months ago, the vast majority were in good health. Some had bouts with cancer and survived. A couple of them were dealing with medical issues such as chemo treatment and COPD. But on average, this is a healthy group of guys.

Now that I am in my 70's, I recognize the blessing of good health. Despite the cancer fight from a few months back, which you'll learn about in subsequent sections, my current health is incredibly good. Thanks to the comfortable south Texas weather, I am able to do a daily walk in Salado Creek Park. Oftentimes, this turns out to be the high point of my day. I do not have any current pressing medical issues. In short, I have nothing to complain about.

I challenge myself to press on with a good attitude, trying to enjoy every new day. During my prime, the term getting lucky had a sexual connotation. Now at old age, getting lucky means you can actually find your car in the parking lot after buying groceries.

As I think about old age, I can't help but think about my immediate relatives. In order, the youngest to die was my father. He was gone by age 60. Next in the longevity track was my paternal grandfather, Christ, who died at age 80. The longest longevity was my maternal grandfather, Hie, who died at age 90. Of no particular relevance was the death of Teddy Roosevelt, who died in his sleep at age 60. He had a history of being tough on his body, including ranch living in North Dakota and his late-life exploration off the Amazon.

One final example of getting lucky is the fact that at age 73, I have two beautiful and impressive lady friends. They are a safe distance apart— Nebraska and. Texas. They are both fun to be with and in their own respective ways, and they keep me on the straight and narrow. I never expected this good fortune at this stage of my life.

When you consider the adventures as told in previous stories, I should never have grown old. Someone in heaven looked after me, and once again, that included *an abundance of good luck.*

Having Kids

A previous story had related some of life's challenges, but this chapter offers nothing but good news, good memories, and again, another example of being blessed by luck.

I pondered back to my first marriage when my wife, at the time, argued the advantages of not having kids. Her common theme seemed to be one of selfishness. There was a lot of emphasis on "me" and children would just be a distraction. They would get in the way, and they would cost a lot of money.

The main reason that the first wife became my ex-wife was that she had herself sterilized while I was deployed to the Pacific Rim. Her decision was made alone, and I was never consulted. In short, she was not the loyal wife she had purported to be. When I realized what she had done, I became depressed because it seemed perfectly normal to wish for a family.

I started to consider a divorce, but I was neither swift nor decisive. Honestly, I was concerned about how much the divorce would cost me and how long it would take to recover. I am ashamed to say I contemplated this decision for seven years—a low point in my life—before I got the nerve to make the divorce decision. When I delivered that divorce statement, I felt like a giant load had been lifted from my shoulders. And so goes another day in married life.

At that point, I had no clue how I would find a family, but at least I had a fresh start to pursue that goal. A fresh start can open up countless possibilities.

I was not divorced long before I met the mother of my children. One of the things that attracted me to her was our common goal of wanting a medium-size family, nor did it hurt that she was a petite little beauty queen.

Not long after, 1984, little Christian came along. Two more children followed in prompt succession in nearly two-year intervals. For some reason, I had this impression that all my kids would be similar, look alike, and act alike. I could not have been more wrong.

My dream of raising a family came true, and I was again a lucky man again.

All I had to do now was to figure out how to raise these kids. I am going to skip the gory details of raising kids in a pressure cooker marriage, but I managed. After about seven years, there was another divorce, and now the challenge went in a different direction. The oldest son made a declaration immediately after the divorce decision. He emphatically said that he did not want to live with his mother because "she is too crazy."

A judge, in his infinite wisdom, determined that the two younger kids would live with their mother. As luck would have it, they lived on the opposite coast, making it difficult for regular visits. The mother's lack of parental cooperation made that task even harder. Consequently, I was only able to see Lauren and Steffen on rare occasions. This was not my idea of how fatherhood was supposed to work.

This all changed in 1997 when I received a call to come pick up the kids; their mother committed suicide. Despite the tragedy of that moment, all of the kids were now together in one location and in my family unit. My new family unit was inchoate, and I realized that I would have my hands full with the task of developing a new family unit.

As an odd side note here, I received an e-mail weeks prior to the suicide that she simply made the statement, "Okay, you win."

My first thought was, "Riddle me this, Batman." I had no idea what her short and cryptic message meant. Now, I think I knew.

So, this is where the full family story actually starts.

I had the good fortune of building a 3-story log home on the north shore of Lake Tahoe. This would be home to the task of raising kids. You can't live around Lake Tahoe without getting into the winter skiing routine. We all skied or participated in some variation of snow sports. It was good clean living, and it included all members of the family.

All the kids went to Incline Village schools. However, the school was a bitter disappointment for the boys and me, as it seemed solely focused on college prep. Neither of the boys had an interest in attending a traditional college, and consequently, they both dropped out. I feared this was the beginning of limited opportunities for both boys. I was wrong.

Because she was a natural in school, Lauren was the exception. She could succeed anywhere, even UCLA. A few years after graduation, she now works for TD Ameritrade, offering financial advice and leading the good life in San Diego.

One of my great joys was watching Lauren turn into a world-class cross-country runner. I used to take her into the Tahoe mountains for training runs. At first, I would run ahead and wait for her. It was not long before she ran ahead and waited for me. About this time, she started to win almost every cross country race she entered. This was at the junior high school level and continued into high school. She was lean and mean and had a determination that was to die for. She told me once that running a good race was a "near-death experience" because you have to push your body and mind as far as it will go.

Her running coach taught her a trick about psyching out the competition by waiting to pass other runners while they were on a hill. When they watched her pass them by, they would lose heart. This is why she would often collapse at the finish line. During the state high school championship meet, she lay in a pile for almost 10 minutes before she could get up. Her efforts and fatigue served her well because, as a freshman, she took second in the state. I was very proud of her accomplishments. She was my overachiever, as seen in the sketch near the top of this section.

Christian, though not interested in academics, quickly got into the high school athletic routine. He seemed to have a fondness for multiple coaches, and that simply moved along the motivation and development. He was #51 linebacker on the football team and when I started to call him BRUISER. He seemed to enjoy punishing the ball carried if and when he made it through the line.

He also wrestled with credentials. He made the regional team as a freshman. The coach said that though he had very few wrestling skills, he was unusually strong for his age and size. So, if you can't outwrestle your opponent, just body slam him into submission.

Steffen was the oddball. He did not like team sports and said that from the beginning. Unfortunately, he was the most athletic of all the kids. He used trick skis, and he used them well. The Incline newspaper got a photo of him in full flight, with Lake Tahoe in the background. The photo made it look like he was jumping into the lake. Without permission or compensation, this photo was used by the newspaper as a promotional push to come to visit Lake Tahoe. I still have that photo framed.

Of all the kids, I believe that Steffen is closest to me in body type and temperament. He has impressed me again as I watch his skills as a new father. It seems that he must have read the good parenting books. He loves to take his kids and family camping even in the dead of winter. You know what they say about camping, you spend a small fortune to live like a homeless person. But they loved it.

My two sons are depicted at the top of the page, Christian on the left and Steffen on the right.

It is easy to classify kids in that age bracket from 0-18. This is the hard-labor portion of raising kids. I did not expect to find the period after age 18 to be so pleasant. I have often said that I enjoy my adult kids more than in the early years. They have good personal characteristics; they are easy to talk to; they seem to support dear old dad.

Other characteristics that I hope they learned from their dad include hard work and loyalty. Both boys have a good track record for finding work, and I assume those characteristics were also noticed by many respective bosses. Lauren has also been successful, finding a job she enjoys and is financially well situated.

In June 2014, I proudly traveled to UCLA to watch the Peanut graduate. I nicknamed my daughter Peanut because she weighs only 110 pounds. Don't let that fool you; she did a tour in the Army and is qualified in five different assault weapons. Pinch me because I think I am dreaming. That little rascal not only graduated but did so with honors.

One thing I have learned along the way is that children from the same parents are not going to be the same. If that were the case, fatherhood would have been boring.

Update from Feb 2018. Yesterday, my sister Carol called to check on me, and we got to discussing kids and grandkids. She reminded me that I was the only male Riersgard out of six children—three from my father's side and three from his brother's side—to produce grandkids with the Riersgard name to carry on. I had not slowed down enough to ponder that unique position, but wait, there could be more. Both Liza, my daughter-in-law, and Steffen are still talking about more kids. They'll all be Riersgards, so who knows where this will end. There is no doubt that I have been blessed. Bring on all the grandchildren this world can produce.

Without any question, *my best stroke of luck* was having three healthy and likable kids who reached adulthood. I enjoy each of them in their own way. Thank you, Lord.

Making the Ranch Better

My life can be broken down into four parts, first was my younger days on the farm and then to college, the second was my 20 years in the Marine Corps, third was my law enforcement career, and finally was my 14 years on this small ranch.

I bought my ranch in 2005. I had big plans to turn this piece of sagebrush property into something that I could enjoy. My original ranch house was built in the 2007-2008 time frame. I had a design concept borrowed by a unique structure in King's Beach, Lake Tahoe.

I had a simple concept of a small and functional home, with just one bedroom. This decision turned out to be a mistake, as will be explained shortly. I also had a fixed amount of money, and building a larger home was not practical at the time. This chapter will focus on the decision to add a bunkhouse close to the original ranch house. The expansion doubled the living space on this property. The above illustration depicts the bunkhouse as the first structure, the ranch house as the second, and the bathhouse as the third.

During the seven years of living in this house, I managed to find "Stuff that eventually got in the way and, over time, I realized that I needed to expand.

During this same period, I discovered that many of my adult children actually enjoyed this ranch. Christian and Liza spend a fair amount of time out here. I needed more room to accommodate our guests, even if they are family. Steffen visited slightly less often, and Lauren has her professional career ahead of her, and this ranch is currently low on her priority list.

Along these lines, Christian announced plans to move to the ranch not later than 1 October 2014. This decision was driven by multiple factors. He was tired of working-for-the-man in a high tempo operation where hired help is not often treated well. He and Liza were talking about starting a family and wanting to do this in a slower-paced rural environment. He also wants to be close to the action in case the local saloon comes up for sale. This would allow him to start work the day after we buy the business. The one factor that meant a lot to me is the fact that he feels the old man needs some help in running the ranch. Indeed, I often have heavy lifting chores where I could use his help. He wants to help me at home instead of moving me to a home when I get to that feeble age. I am grateful for this decision. This idea lasted about 3-4 months before they moved back to Reno. His priorities were still evolving.

When Christian announced he wanted to move here, he said he would be willing to move into the small well house so the spare bedroom could remain available for guests. I proposed that a spare bedroom should get the maximum use, and therefore, I invited them to move into that bigger space. That space was completed before they moved out from Reno.

One of my lucky blessings was the fact that my father kept the mineral rights to his farm when he sold the land and farm proper. As luck had it, our property was right on top of the Bakken Oil Patch, one of the largest oil reserves in America. This reality meant that Hess Oil Company, who owned the Bakken Oil Patch was sending monthly oil royalty checks

When the oil money news arrived, I decided to make the new house addition a priority. It took nearly two years of oil savings to get enough money to start the project. I still had some home equity credit in my Wells Fargo account, and I felt I should have enough money to pay the $156,xxx price tag. The actual cost ran higher because I added a few upgrades, not on the contractor's estimate sheet.

The bunkhouse, depicted at the top of this story, is on the left. The ranch house is in the middle, and the bathhouse is on the right.

I contacted the same contractor that built the main house and had good intentions of having this structure built during the spring of 2013. Unfortunately, the contractor lost his framing crew, and he was unable to build on my schedule. This was okay because it gave me more time to save money to ensure I was close to covering the construction cost.

Thanks to some arm-twisting, the contractor managed to talk the previous framing crew into a return visit from Boise. Dave and Eric were favorite guys on the first project and even more so on the second project. This was a father and son team. I was so happy to have their professional framing work; I bribed them with hot coffee in the morning and cold beer in the late afternoon. We also had a series of conversations around the dining table in the evenings after they knocked off work. In short, we got along just great.

Later, I took four yellow buckets and laid out a footprint that I thought would define my new bunkhouse. I had two priorities in the design plan. First, I needed two more bedrooms. Second, I needed an office so I could move my papers from the dining room table, and I also needed a more suitable location for bills and ranch records.

The footprint location was Northeast of the ranch house. Because of the geology and geography of the building site, the new structure would be pushed partway over the ledge; half sat on flat ground, and the other half hung out over the edge. This created extra work and strain on the backhoe operator who had to break enough rock so a stem wall could be poured. The stem wall would support that portion hanging over the edge.

Eventually, the design evolved. Though I felt that an office would be beneficial, I designed an oversized room so I could do other things with the space. The other things included an 8' dining table used for holiday dinners. It was designed to have a comfortable area in the SE corner with a wood-burning stove, easy chairs, and a sleeper sofa, so in a pinch, this space could serve as a third bedroom.

The bonus feature of this addition is a 56' x 12' attic storage area, which was badly needed. Just look at the mezzanine in the shop. It was overflowing with stuff, stuff that never managed to get thrown away. Some people call it clutter. It is filled with excess stuff from the 5,000 square foot house at Lake Tahoe and includes books, small furniture, clothing, etc. Some of those boxes were packed so long ago; I don't even remember what's in them.

A late design conversation between myself and the contractor concluded that interior attic stairs would not be practical if I moved a lot of large stuff. Consequently, we agreed to design a metal staircase on the south exterior end of the structure. This would allow a more comfortable transport of junk to the attic.

It would have been nice to pay the extra money to have this attic space finished, but our construction costs were starting to climb, and I needed to save somewhere. Perhaps this step can be managed down the road.

On the other hand, I clearly had enough excess furniture that I could outfit these new spaces with existing items. Over time, I accumulated other furniture items, such as multiple large bookcases and nice bed frames. This means the new rooms were quickly furnished.

One design feature changed due to cost consideration, was the solar power system. I had worked with Aspen Electric out of Reno to provide independent power via solar. Their estimate came to $27K. The contractor reminded me that he could pull power from under the main house for around $2K. The price difference presented an easy choice to change my mind on solar power.

Years later, I planned to put the entire ranch under solar power. The early estimate was around $50K, .s less than double the estimate for just the bunkhouse addition.

While some savings were factored in, I decided to add air conditioning, though I failed to take this step on the ranch house.

After paying the contractor, I added a couple more items to the remodel. This includes the incinerator toilet for $1800 and a gun safe for$1500. Yes, all ranches need gun safes.

When the structure was framed, my son and I had a joking conversation. We agreed that the building looked kind of like a motel, including an attic upstairs for Mrs. Bates. Christian suggested that it would be cute to name it *The Bates Motel*. I agreed. Now, when you visit, you'll see a large wall sign that says Bates Motel on the front exterior.

As I finished the rough framing inspection, I awaited the insulation and sheetrock steps. The day after the last inspection, I drove the ranch truck and trailer to Reno. I picked up eight windows from Eagle Window and a pallet and half,7200 pounds, of cherry hardwood flooring. Combined, it certainly created a full and heavy load. I was glad to install good quality Anderson windows rather than the cheap vinyl windows suggested by the contractor. I ended up installing the hardwood flooring on my own.

Eventually, the construction was eventually finished, and the end product was even more wonderful than I expected. On a typical day, the bunkhouse gets as much activity as the main house. Expanding the ranch infrastructure was a good decision, and helps to explain why my fourth phase of life has been one more example of practical changes and *good luck.*

Cows Not Condos

Some years ago, I saw the bumper sticker that said Cows not Condos. It was comfortably placed on an older ranch pickup truck. It represented part of a rural push to protect our open spaces and not ruin those parts of northern Nevada that have hosted traditional ranches for nearly a hundred years. Ranches are one thing, and medium-size cities are another. During my time before I bought my ranch, both Reno and Boise showed signs of rapid growth. Las Vegas had already been lost. Las Vegas growth will not stop until they run out of water, and that is sooner than most residents want to admit.

I can't seem to find any condos outside my ranch house window. It should probably stay that way because I have BLM land on two sides and a large working ranch on a third side. I don't expect that this neighbor has any plan to subdivide. My space should be protected from any future condo development.

Since my earliest days on this ranch property, I have appreciated the ranch lifestyle and the beautiful views from every direction. I spend the most time on the front porch, looking down on the green Muffler Meadow with a year-round stream running down through that green patch.

Now I can look through the trees in the front yard all the way to the large trees at the Old Mill Ranch. This will always be one of the best views on any property.

To put the current view into perspective, I think back on the decades when the only view out my window was the apartment next door or the house that was built way too close to my window.

More specifically, today, June 20th, 2014, at 6:45 a.m. I take a fresh cup of coffee outside to enjoy in the swing chair. I have my front yard garden in the foreground and the meadow in the background. As we approach the summer solstice, the sun is just coming over the east bank of Martin Creek. The current sunrise location is well up into the rock canyon, to my left. This view is a reminder that I have had some success in getting the front yard landscape established. Initially, all of my work seemed to provide a horizontal reward versus a vertical reward. In the beginning, there was no height to the shrubs and trees. Now, nine years into the evolution, both trees and shrubs are getting mature and tall.

This front yard garden was planted on a rock platform, the same rock platform upon which the house was built). In some cases, I could break up the rocks to provide room for topsoil. In other cases, I used medium size rocks to build beds. This approach also provided room for soil and manure. Only in the south corner is the luxury of normal soil. The best example is the honey locust tree that is growing just fine. Also, the cherry trees just outside the block wall are in natural soil. Now the soil has been augmented many times and is rich enough to host earthworms. This is a far cry from the original clay and rock that would never permit such worms.

Once I complained that the bedrock, which typifies the west bank of the creek, where my house and yard are located, made my life difficult. I made this complaint to the fellow who had to take his backhoe and smash into the rocks to create an opening for the house foundation. His reply was that if it were not for these rocks, the entire west bank of Martin Creek would have washed into the meadow floor about seventeen million years ago. He suggested I stop complaining.

I have learned that the summer conditions in late June, July, and August are hard on my landscape. I almost need to have water running continually to keep the landscape alive. The same is true for the vegetable garden, the orchard, the many trees at the beach, and the vineyard. This is an example of the little, simple chores that give me purpose in these days of ranch living.

During December '17 and January '18, we had such a mild winter that the day time temp was around 50 degrees. This allowed for morning coffee on the front porch even into January.

Eventually, the weather pattern changed to traditional winter by the end of February.

Cows are the mainstay of the community of Paradise Valley. Many large cattle ranches establish the fabric of the ranching community. Other properties produce large amounts of alfalfa hay. This product seems to truck westbound to the larger dairy farms in Northern California. Cows can be labor-intensive. When they are out grazing, they are mostly self-sufficient. When it comes time for branding, vaccination, castration, preg-checks and the many other tasks, extra help is required. In the valley is a wonderful tradition of ranchers helping ranchers. Sometimes the work also includes non-ranchers such as myself. The working crews during these seasonal events will often number from a dozen to twice that amount.

The sketch at the top depicts the annual fall cattle drive from the Forest Service grazing allotments in the mountains, past my house on the way to the respective ranches on the valley floor.

As luck has it, some of the ranches have families that are made up of only daughters, sometimes providing an interesting challenge of how the ranch will be handed down to the next generation. Another challenge to ranching is that most large ranches can only survive when there are ranch hands willing to help with the daily chores. Generally, these workers are very dedicated and hard-working individuals or families. A long tradition of vaqueros or buckaroos fills this void. In Paradise Valley, most all of the larger ranches have buckaroos on the payroll.

A variety of concerns exist for this rural community, but we remain free from signs of commercial development, and thus, the many ranches should be stable for many years ahead.

All in all, this is a great place in a great location, and there are no condos in the future. Long live the established ranches and the annual cattle drives. *Long live this good luck.*

Riersgard Family History

The sketch at the left is a special recognition of my Norwegian grandmother, Thea. She was about as original as you can get for a tough Scandinavian woman.

The idea of seriously undertaking a research effort on the family history first took shape after the 2015 family reunion. So far, this was the one and only large-scale family reunion. A second reunion may take place in 2020, depending on the Coronavirus.

The family history idea took shape as my cousin Linda, and I decided to make this a joint effort. One generation prior, my father made a feeble effort to research family history. This included notes from his brother, Ken, who traveled back to where our Norwegian family farm was located. It was probably Ken who managed to get his hands on a printed short version of the Slekten Reiersgarden OG Liabraten, Fla I Hallingdal 1595 to 1962 history. This came from Norway and had been translated into English. This account provided some badly needed information on my family. I learned my family name started as Liabraten and later changed to Reiersgard. There is no indication of why this change took place.

My father's efforts to work on history did not bear much fruit. Unlike the present day, where the Internet provides easy access to research, my dad had good intentions but was only able to share limited information. Later research indicated that some of his research was valid, and some was not.

So, prior to the efforts of Linda and myself, the family tree was only a couple of branches high.

As an example, I have recently found a cousin in nearby Houston. His grandmother is the sister of my grandfather. Her name is Gertrude, Goer, Gor, or Goldie, depending. She came to American with her older brother Reir. She was only 15 at the time. My father indicated that she married well and was a prominent person in Minneapolis. Nothing more was learned about her adult life except that she was buried in San Benito, north of Brownsville, Texas. We believe that Goldie may have been an early snowbird from Minnesota. If and when I can have a personal visit with her off-spring, Ralph, I hope to fill in some of the blanks.

My efforts started with Ancestry.com, and I started an on-line family tree. The tree grew slowly. Some of the blind contacts were helpful, and other contacts never responded. However, one contact was very noteworthy. That contact came from Dennis Reiersgard, who lives at Whidbey Island, Washington. His first contact was a blunt statement that he and I shared the same grandfather. My first reaction was one of simple disbelief. This could not be possible as I personally knew my grandfather, Christ O. Riersgard, and he only had two sons. The oldest was Ken, and the younger son, Raymond, was my father. My reply to Dennis may have been too curt. He came back with a copy of the birth certificate of his father, Milton, and sure enough, it listed my grandfather as the father and Ann-Marie Reiersgard as the mother. I turned to Linda to see if she could shed any light on this new revelation. The birth date on the certificate was 1910, so that was a starting point. Linda found out that Christ sailed back to Norway to recover two domestic workers from the family farm, one male and one female. The female was Ann-Marie. They were briefly together in Minnesota in the right time frame, so I went to Dennis and welcomed him to the family. We are slowly getting to know our new-found cousin.

I have since departed Ancestry. It seemed that this source had served its purpose, and not much else could be learned.

I was still a little uncertain, so I asked Dennis for a photo. Most folks would say that he and I look like brothers.

Back to the family tree. Another cousin, Phil, was able to find a large chunk of the family tree. We plugged that into what we already had. Thanks to this new info, we have a tree pushing out to the year 763 A.D. This new information included a section for Sigurd II, 1133-1155, listed as King of Norway. The first reaction was to assume that this was a mistake or a misprint. Undaunted, I put that name into a Google search. To my surprise, an 8-page history popped up from Wikipedia detailing the family and battle history of this relative. This account then pushed family detail to his father, who was also a king. And so, it went with the research for eight generations. Perhaps the most noteworthy was King Magnus, who was the last Viking warrior King. For kings, who were also warriors, the life expectancy was not long. Sigurd was killed by age 22. Magnus was killed in his early 30's.

Fast forward from 1155 A.D. to 2006. The first date was the death of King Sigurd II. The second date was the year that I read the book, *Giants in the Earth*.

For any good Norwegian interested in what the early migration into the Dakotas was like, the book, *Giants in the Earth*, a saga of the prairie, by O.E. Rolvaag is a must-read. There has been some debate if this book should be called a Norwegian classic or an American classic. The author is Norwegian, but the story setting is South Dakota.

It matters not, because it is a classic story of high hopes and major setbacks in the quest to find some land and make a better living. As was the case in my family, the Norwegian immigrant, Per Hansa, was the driving force in pushing westward and building his homestead on raw prairie. In the case of my family, the support structure was there with the Norwegian wife. In the case of Per

Hansa, he had the constant challenge of dealing with his wife, Beret, who had severe reservations about this new life.

It may be safe to say that she had mental health issues that made Per Hansa's life more difficult. I feel fortunate in that I spent some of my early years on my Grandfather's homestead in North Dakota. I got to experience first-hand the austere living with very little money. Consequently, nothing was wasted.

He started with a couple of draft horses, a few milk cows, some pigs, and chickens, just like in the old country. The biggest difference was that many of the immigrants came from small farms with tiny acreage in Norway. Now they were getting homestead rights to a minimum of 160 acres. In many cases, they acquired more acres. These stories of free land were getting back to Norway, so the migration continued into the early 1900s.

The sketch below illustrates the only source of regular income from my grandparent's homestead. My grandfather's name is on this crème can, but it was his wife, Thea, who did the work to fill the can with crème and transport it to the rail depot, long since gone, at Manitou. The GN on the tag indicates the Great Northern Railroad.

The only spending money that Grandma Thea ever had was from the sale of crème. Each day she would milk the cows and carry the milk to the separator. There the crème would be pulled off. It would be stored in a crème can with Grandpa's name on the outside. Every few weeks, she would transport that can to the rail station in Manitou. It would be picked up by a small train called the Dinky. Somewhere in this process, she would receive a small check.

In *Giants in the Earth*, it was noted that fellow immigrants that came from Hallingdal Valley were called Hallings. My grandfather was a Hallings.

During the course of the joint research effort, Linda found a story of incredible efficiency. This had to do with the multiple legs of the journey from the old country into South Minnesota, which seemed to be a gathering location for our side of the family. After years of migration, someone made an effort to make this journey easier. This step was taking place between 1866 and 1920. At this time, large numbers of people were leaving Norway on steamships. It seems that most were sailing to Hull, England. From there they traveled to Liverpool, England. From there, they sailed to either the U.S. or Canada. The steamship option reduced the journey from three months to only two or three weeks.

Apparently, the standard route to Minnesota started with a rail trip to Oslo, then a boat trip to Hull, England, then another train ride across to Liverpool, then a 2-3-week steamship to Quebec, then a rail ride to Minneapolis. These five legs were eventually included in one master ticket. This step made the trip more efficient, and considering language problems on the second half made the trip easier. We have no way of knowing what this master ticket would have cost.

For Riersgard family members, most seemed to gather in places like Breckenridge and Brooten, Minnesota. It was Linda that pieced together this story about one ticket from start to finish. There is no explanation why so many Riersgards sailed to Quebec as opposed to Ellis Island. It could be that Quebec offered a less hectic port of entry than New York.

Not once did my Grandfather ever explain that his side of the family came from Norwegian royalty. My guess is that he had no clue about King Sigurd II or King Magnus. When you are struggling to make a subsistence living, royalty does not matter.

In the interest of remembering the family history, my oldest son has selected the middle name of Magnus for his second son as a tribute to the last Viking warrior king. After Magnus, the kings decided not to venture into battle. Consequently, they lived longer.

As a parallel to the above Magnus story, I am proud that my second son named his first daughter, Thea, after his great grandmother. This is an example of the little things that make a father proud. I have long encouraged my kids to pick names from the family tree. Now they are doing exactly that.

These above stories from the homestead will never be reflected in the family tree, but they are essential for the real family history. Perhaps this book can memorialize some of these facts for my kids and grandkids.

Completing the family tree is difficult, and major sections of the tree have little or no detail. If you are not a king, you don't show up on a Google search. However, this is where Cousin Linda came in. She had a knack of digging into church records, ship manifests, census records, and the like. This detail helped to make the new oral history more interesting.

For example, Linda found Guri Arnesdatter Hoftun (1656-1757), and the dates illustrate that she lived to the age of 101. During her life span, she mothered 18 children. So, she spent most of her adult life in the perpetual state of pregnancy. Do you suspect that she was one tough gal? Since most farms in Norway were very small, it would be interesting to know where she put all of these kids. And, how do you feed that many children?

Another female from the tree became pregnant thanks to a Norwegian soldier. The church influence was very strong at this point. According to church rules, she had to stand in front of the entire congregation and confess her sins. Can you imagine the trauma of that event? As a point of interest here, the father was not required to do the same. He was exempt because he worked for the King, and had soldier status. Later the church relaxed this rule.

As one piece of evidence led to another, we learned about the Wends. Oral history indicates that the Wends were both fair-haired as well as dark-skinned. Again, oral history seems to indicate that the family has dark-skinned relatives from the Wend connection.

I should share that there was limited influence from the Wends. The Wends were a nomadic Germanic tribe that found their way into Norway and England. They briefly show up in the family tree with a female by the name of Edla Wend (954-1010). Her parents were listed as Edward of Wends (931). There was no detail on the mother, and there was no death date.

Cousin Linda and I made a brief effort to research the significance of the Wends but did not find much detail. We don't know if there were of a farming background or a seafaring background. Considering where they came from, it was probably the former. My DNA already has a connection to Eastern Europe but that was on my maternal side. Those Wends that were connected with the ancient Goths were remarkable for their tall stature, pale complexion, and blonde hair. Research indicates that they were mainly Slavs with a connection to Bulgaria. The longer research indicates that they were dispersed all over the map.

The final side story here is the fact that my DNA indicates a 2% Iberian Peninsula, Spain, or Portugal. I have a theory, but it is only partially based on facts. The first fact is that the Vikings established a logistics base in Southern Spain in the coastal city of Cadiz. Cadiz is close to the

Straits of Gibraltar and is considered to be a tourist hot spot today. This base was established in 844. At this time, the Vikings were known for their slave trade on the open market further into the Mediterranean. The second fact is the slave trade, which included both men and women. Based on portrayals on the History channel, the Vikings were also known to retain some of these female foreign prisoners for return trips to Norway. Once these ladies were established in the Viking community, they would often marry the men. This might explain my 2% DNA. I would assume that this eventual marriage connection would be helped along provided the slave was a good-looking woman.

As a side note, I joined the Reno chapter of Sons of Norway. We would meet monthly. During my time there, there was a lot of emphasis on genealogy. One fellow, who had a better hard copy of his family history, also pushed his tree to the same point that I had researched.

His detail on certain battles, especially in England, was much stronger than anything I could muster. He pointed out that those of us who had trees going back as far as his and mine had a good probability that all Norwegians were related. He noted that in the 763 A.D. time frame, the total population of Norway was less than one million. This supported his theory that we Norwegians were all related early on.

Also, remember that what was called Norway from the Viking era was much different from current Norway. The age of the Vikings represented a portion of Norway that was limited to the western one-third of the current Norwegian boundary on the Atlantic side. It followed south in a district called Bestfold, towards Oslo. It should be noted that in the early stages, Oslo had nothing to do with the Viking nation.

"The system of kings in Viking-Age Scandinavia was confused and convoluted, and kings were rarely supreme national leaders." page 49, *The Viking Warrior* by Ben Hubbard.

One advantage of the detail gathered was that strong accounts could be put together, especially in the most recent generations. This came in handy when we found cousin Dennis. I was able to share a long history of our grandfather. Until this point, he knew nothing about his grandfather, Christ Riersgard.

If there is any confusion on the spelling of the last name, it started out as the longer version Reiersgard. Christ shortened that to Riersgard later in his life. So, Dennis has the longer spelling, and I have the shorter spelling.

I was aware that at some point, I would no longer be a member of Ancestry.com, and thus my on-line family tree would be removed from my access. So, I bought large white poster boards, and now the tree has been hand-drawn so that it is memorialized in a tangible form. This copy will be shared and discussed at the next reunion. I assume I will hand over these poster boards to my oldest son.

I am thankful and *lucky to have Viking blood in my system.* I am especially thankful for the eight generations of Viking kings in the family tree. One of the more famous was Magnus the Barefoot. My newest grandson shares his middle name with King Magnus.

With each new generation of kids and grandkids, the amount of Norwegian blood gets smaller and smaller.

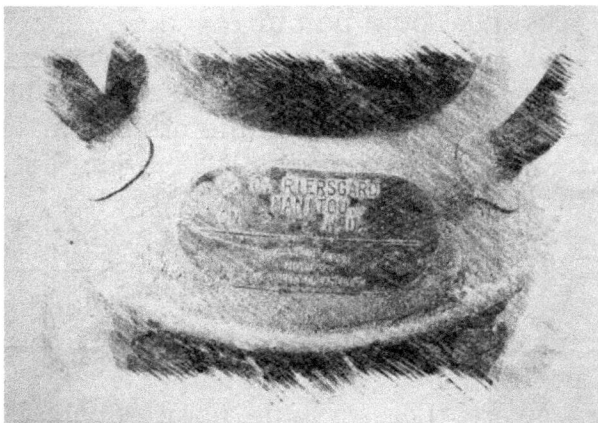

Reflections

I am sitting around the ranch house, watching a Fleetwood Mac DVD concert. Near the end, Stevie Nicks sang a song about "Changes," and it prompted the idea of putting down some thoughts about my personal changes as the life cycle was moving forward. The sketch at the top of this story represents me and my age at the time I was drafting this chapter.

As I think ahead, I hope that I can share a picture that will prompt joy and satisfaction regarding the purpose and value of my life. After all, this long life has provided everything I had hoped for and more. The illustration depicted above is an example of sharing a picture and a key part of my reflections.

As a poor country farm boy, my only wish was to escape the farm and explore the bigger world. I accomplished that goal and then some. At that time, I had no idea of the roller coaster ride that life would present. I had no idea how many times my heart would be broken or my pulse quickened. Accordingly, I had no idea of the many personal challenges that would confront me. But in the final analysis, there is no escaping the fact that the good outweighed the bad. Perhaps, God threw in the rough times so I could better appreciate the good times all the more. Or perhaps it was simply a way of testing me.

Let me pause at a turning point for this country boy. The year was 1961, and I was 15 years old. This is old enough for a farm boy to carry his own weight and serve as a functioning farmhand. As such, I had been assigned hay stack duty in the middle of August. August is one of the hottest months in the North Dakota hay fields. It was not unusual for the midday temperature to hit 100 degrees.

My specific job was to groom the stack. My father would dump loose hay on the ground, and then I was to move the hay in such a manner that it was now flat enough to build upon. So, the next load of hay would come on top of the last load that I had groomed. And so, it goes, the stack increases in height until the tractor loader can no longer reach any higher.

As described well in the book, *Making Hay*, by Verlny Klinkenborg, "If you set out to make a haystack using conventional agricultural implements, the height of the stack rapidly out-scales them, and you confront the fundamental problem of haystack building—getting the hay on top of an ever-growing pile."

The burden of finding a solution here was left to my farmer father. He seemed to know what to do to build a stack and keep me busy.

It is hard work moving hay with a pitchfork, especially when the base you're standing on never seems to be sturdy or close to solid. Add the fact that when I did farm work, I hardly ever wore a shirt. Consequently, my torso skin color was the same tone as a dark brown beer bottle. Loose hay comes with stickers and other things that tended to scratch and itch the skin of my bare torso. At the time, this was not a big deal, just an occupational reality.

When my father determined that the stack is complete, he'd bring the hay loader abeam the stack so I can step off the stack and find my balance on the loader. Then, it is time to start the process all over again.

One day in August, I am nearing the top of the stack when my eye catches a small movement on the horizon. It starts out as a large dot, but it is clearly moving in my direction and was getting larger quickly. Soon, it is apparent that I am looking at an Air Force fighter jet, I believed it to be an F-105.

I am certain that the jet pilot spotted me on top of that stack, and he was going to make my day. He buzzed the stack at approximately the same height that I was standing on the stack. He passed about 30 yards abeam at probably 250 knots.

As he passed, I offered up a wave of awe and envy. Maybe it was also a wave of humble appreciation because he had just made my day. He returned the favor with a wave from the cockpit. He was so close that he blew off part of the hay that I had just groomed. But that was okay because I felt that I had just been given my own personal air show. As I found out later, his route was on a high speed, low-level training course out of the Minot Air Force Base.

My father witnessed this event from the ground, but he had no idea what was going through my head at that moment. What was going on in my head, I would call a eureka moment. From that moment forward, I was now determined to grow up to be a military pilot. From his perspective, my father had just lost his hired man.

My mind was no longer on the haystack but rather playing with the vision of the day when I could strap into a military aircraft. This was my childhood seminal moment.

Fast forward to late January 1969, eight years later. The farm boy now nears the end of Naval Flight training in Pensacola, Florida. As I start to gain confidence in flying a T-28, I could probably use the term cocky. One day a flight of four left home base and flew out to an aircraft carrier for what was called Carrier Qualifications.

On that day, we took turns making trapped landings, trying to catch the 3-wire on the flight deck. This was a moment of complete exhilaration and satisfaction. I have often thought of the time gap between 1961 and 1969. So much had happened, and my wildest dream came true. I traded in haystacks for military aircraft. Life seemed to be treating me just fine. Maybe this was another example of <u>good luck</u> along the way.

What does it feel like to land on the carrier? I have heard it described as having an orgasm and a car accident at the same time. I think that is a good description.

Regarding my escape from the farm, the Marine Corps was my ticket, literally around the world a couple of times. Thanks to spending too much time on a helicopter carrier, I have sailed the seven seas, and I served on five continents. Some of these spots were simply sojourns in faraway lands. I flew large helicopters from South Vietnam, and I flew support for the President.

Fast forward to February 2020 in San Antonio, Texas. I am attending the very large rodeo, and I'm in awe of the size of this event. There were brief periods in between events when I had time to visit the vendor building.

During one such visit, I found a painting by Bruce Greene called *When Freedom isn't Free.* It is a touching scene where a young Marine waits at the bus station. His father sits next to him with a lost look and no conversation. The Marine sits next to the family cow dog, and his hands hold a brown bag with a lunch that his mother most likely provided. Close by is the quint-essential seabag indicating he was headed back to his Marine home base. You would have to believe that this pending bus trip is one step closer to going to Vietnam.

The cowboy father in this painting is in the process of losing his strong and strapping ranch hand, just as my father lost his farm hand son.

With almost more careers than I can count, all I want on my tombstone is U.S. Marine. Almost everything I really needed to know about life was learned there. One evening, I had the pleasure of attending a USMC Birthday Ball in San Francisco. I was the guest of John Staples, my former Vietnam hootch-mate.

The MC for the evening was George Shultz, the Secretary of State under President Reagan, from 1982 to 1989. While he served the President, he once said that everything that he learned that was important, he learned in the Marine Corps. Remember, he was a Princeton graduate before he joined the Marines. Things like loyalty—Semper Fi—hard work and taking care of your troops were infused into my head at an early stage.

Never in my adult life did I rub elbows with such sharp, fellows. They were all inspired, young, and adventurous men. It was not just the folks that make up the Corps, but also the history and tradition of a proud organization. A Marine buddy recently explained that Marines don't know what the word quit means, even if a Marine might not know what a bunch of other words mean. The bottom line is that we are all proud to call ourselves MARINES.

Regarding the adventure of flying a helo for 22 years, almost everything that could possibly happen to a helo pilot happened to me. The 22 years include 20 with the USMC and two years with the Washoe County Sheriff's Office. It was the little things like being shot down, surviving a night time mid-air crash, way too many medevacs, and trying to land on a helo carrier in the Indian Ocean with 60' waves crashing over the flight deck.

In this last example, the fleet commander needed a helo to track and photo a Russian spy vessel that was harassing our small battle group. No one wanted to fly this mission, considering the rough seas. The vast majority of my fellow pilots were circumspect. Then along came Daryl, and he said, "Hell yes, I'll go."

It reminds me of the quote from E. Gordon Liddy, "that which does not kill me makes me stronger." In fairness to these stories, I was always willing to take a calculated risk. In my case, most of these risks had a happy ending.

Perhaps this story compares my decision-making skills with that of a squirrel preparing to cross a road.

We were Modloc (modified location) in the Indian Ocean as part of the possible rescue force, in connection with the hostage rescue effort in Iran. This is the same Indian Ocean where I described landing on a carrier during high seas.

By the time my military helo chapter was coming to a close, I decided it was time to slow down and pursue my other dream of having a family. Granted, I got a late start, but that may have been a blessing in disguise. I was blessed

with three free-spirited and healthy kids—
Christian the bruiser, Steffen the tender-heart
bear, and Lauren, my little peanut—who have
repaid me ten-fold. Life also provided a
stepdaughter Sylvia who turned out fine.

Let me tell you the story of how children came
into my life. My first marriage seemed normal,
except the wife said she wanted children then
changed her mind. So, the only way a family was
going to happen was to move on and find a new
wife. I would have to describe this first divorce
as another example of good luck.

While that second marriage was best described
as a wild ride, it did produce three wonderful kids
just as we planned.

The wild ride was associated with some
untreated mental health issues. So once again, the
divorce was an example of good luck, for which
I'm forever grateful because if I waited too long, I
would also exhibit mental health problems.

It was after the second marriage I started
looking at the benefit of being a serious
bachelor. You may have heard that the definition
of a bachelor is a guy who never made the same
mistake once.

Any reflection on my part would be incomplete
if I did not take a few minutes to pay tribute to
my father. In addition to my words at the front
dedication, I can say that in a world full of
dysfunctional parents, my sisters and I were
blessed with a one of a kind dad.

He not only raised his children, but he also took time to befriend and shelter my sister's friend Jane. Jane will be forever grateful for the role he played. Another female friend of my sister's, Bobbi, still shares fond memories of hanging out at the bar with my parents, everyone smoking and joking. These social settings were a lot of fun and brought back great memories.

I missed many of these evenings, for, at this point, I was off being a Marine. Oddly enough, two gals that spent time with my father are the same two gals who are in my life in the *Final Chapter.*

My father's role was just one more example of being a lucky guy. I will probably never figure out the odds of these two ladies, both having a connection to my father. As I reflect on my life, it is such a puzzle that I ended up with two women in my life that are so special and yet come from the same general location that I grew up in. So, I don't misrepresent myself here, the two women have different roles and certainly are not both romantic partners. You'll learn more about them in a subsequent chapter.

After umpteen careers—military pilot, law enforcement pilot, Pentagon staff officer, Congressional testimony writer, aviation security consultant, deputy sheriff, school teacher, state trooper, outlaw, wildland firefighter, Forest Service biological technician—it was time to go after one more challenge.

I was new to ranch development when I received a phone call. I had an offer to work for the U.S. Forest Service as a crew boss for a weed crew. The weed crew worked to control noxious weeds that infest the beauty of the national forest. This was appealing because the national forest was out my back gate, and I had a yen to discover these 330,000 acres. Part of the deal was to get certified as a wildland firefighter and receive a qualification identification called a red card. To achieve that qualification, I needed to attend a large class at a special school. As you may know, most of these firefighters are younger men, probably in their 20's. I'm their antithesis as a 60-year-old grey beard. After a stand-up and sit-down survey, it turned out that I was the oldest student by far.

I went to work in the forest with a crew of four people, two trucks, and four quads. We ventured into the wildest parts of the forest doing our job. At this point, my theory in life about vitality was either use it or lose it.

At the beginning of this missive, I made reference to changes, and of course, changes are inevitable as time passes. My life was still an example of changes, even as I watched my children grow into adulthood. I could also see the rapid changes as they added on years.

Once upon a time, I recall reading that the lad who never left home can write a book, but it would only be one chapter. Those who left home and did many things can write a longer story. And here I am writing bits and pieces of my life story.

In my case, the biggest changes were yet to come. After 14 years of hard work developing a ranch from scratch, I had reached the decision that the ranch would stay in the family forever. I even put this language into my will. My children all supported my idea.

Then along came a divorce, cancer, and the dull realization that I was not getting any younger. While these above factors all look to be negative, they may have come at me in a manner that I needed to make a major life change. Oscar Wilde once said, "Whenever people agree with me, I always feel I must be wrong." I am not sure how many folks, friends, or family, agree with me on this radical decision change, but I did realize that I needed to make this decision based upon my own factors.

The change to which I refer is the reality check that I needed to get rid of the ranch and move to a warmer climate. This decision did not come easy. But when the decision was finally made, it was time to get to work and sell the place and liquidate all the vehicles, tractors, quads, trailers, and tools. I thought this would be long and painful, but in reality, the liquidation went much quicker than expected.

Even the ranch sale came quicker than expected. The bad news is that when it was time to move off the place, I am at the weakest point in my cancer treatment to date, more on that in the final chapter. The week prior to moving, I was in the Reno hospital with multiple complications from chemo. I did not have the strength to participate in moving furniture and personal effects, so my three kids rallied and did the heavy lifting for me. This was early April 2019. My stuff went to a storage unit in Reno. When the time was right, my stuff would move to south Texas.

My job was to finish my chemo treatment and head to Texas to start a new life. I could not do this until Dr. Singh said I was free of cancer, and that came during early July 2019. By 9 July, I watched Reno get smaller in the rear-view mirror as the long drive to South Texas began.

So, even as I recount these pieces of reflections, I am keenly aware that *good fortune and good luck have followed me* through the best of times and the worst of times.

How Did I Find San Antonio?

The time frame is late October 2019. I have been in San Antonio (S.A.) for many months now, and I'm often asked why I chose this city.

I generally hesitate in my answer because I don't have a clear-cut response to that fair question.

A year before I was operating a ranch in northern Nevada. I had yet to receive my cancer diagnosis, but it was soon to arrive. Now, I am enjoying a nice home here in southern Texas.

What happened?

There were a series of life-changing events that unfolded about one year ago. I already knew that the wife had abandoned the marriage and was preparing to file for divorce. I was soon to get my cancer news. I finally recognized that I was 72 years old and not getting any younger or stronger. When I factored these three things together, it was easy to conclude that I needed a change. So, the question was what kind of change would be in order.

In David Brook's recent book, *The Second Mountain*, on page 39, he explains, "A lot is gained simply by going into a different physical place. You need to taste and touch and feel your way towards a new way of being. And there are huge benefits leaving the center of things and going off into the margins." A change of scenery may even change some luck. Still getting lucky and staying lucky.

The idea of finding a new and different place was a centerpiece in the back of my brain. I did not yet know where I would go; I just knew a change needed to happen. The quest for a new place was described on my Facebook Page as Plan-B.

I actually started a pro/con list of issues important in my life and then imposed this process on different geographic locations. Early on, I considered: North Dakota, staying close to Reno, going to a warmer climate, remaining close to family and friends, or moving closer to an old friend named Bobbi.

As I struggled with these diverse options, I knew that finding warmer winters was going to be important, and that started to narrow my list. I have envied my friends Sheila and Larry, who winter on the Baja Peninsula each winter season. I took out an old atlas and drew a latitude line from west to east, and it ran from San Felipe, Mexico, and concluded in southern Texas. I remembered that my parents would sometimes winter with their friends Lloyd and Evelyn in Brownsville, Texas. Later I learned that Grandpa Christ's sister, Goer, was buried in San Benito, located just north of Brownsville. Texas seemed like a good starting point. Housing prices were affordable, and Brownsville was an attractive location, within sight of the Rio Grande River. The best house I found an old Spanish mission-style, was within throwing distance of the Mexican border. Ultimately, I was not sure moving to this region was the best choice due to the current immigration climate. About this time in my search, a friend emailed me and warned about the crime rate. The more I researched this spot, the less appeal it had.

So, with a continued focus on southern Texas, I started to house-shop, via the internet, in Corpus Christi. After all, this was a Navy town where young jet pilots went to train. As soon as this idea generated some steam, my friend Terry called to ask how I was doing and what my plans were. Terry previously lived in Corpus. When I mentioned that I was considering Corpus, he said, "Daryl, we have to talk." Terry explained that I would be bored after one week because there was nothing to do. He suggested a larger city, perhaps a college town with social life, pubs, live music, etc.

This prompted me to search near-by San Antonio, and many positive factors came to light. I promptly found a wonderful real estate agent by the name of Jean. She and I worked together to find a future home. The search was superficial until I actually landed in S.A. There is a big change from window shopping on the internet and actually walking into a prospective new home.

A move to anywhere does not make sense or does not satisfy unless your new destination provides a home that works. Jean and I looked at approximately 14 homes, and the right one did not present itself until 29 July. My new home is a Mediterranean style with many upgrades. My first impression when I walked in the door was, "This is the place." The second impression was the same, and so was the third. I knew I had my answer. The house is in a good neighborhood with most essential services within a few blocks or a few miles.

Since most services are close by, I could justify buying a Vespa scooter. This takes the load off the Tundra truck, which has seen many miles and has poor gas mileage with city driving.

The worst part about moving so far away was that I would have to start over finding new friends and the reality that I was now a long way from my children and grandchildren. Starting over also meant finding new services like a doctor (via the VA), a new dentist, a church, etc.

My pro/con list got much shorter when I focused on climate. That factor soon eliminated N.D., Reno, and Nebraska. Friends had told me that S.A. was a military town and very friendly. S.A. had a warm winter climate but was still out of the hurricane alley. Texas had already gained the reputation as a favorable relocation site, especially for people fed up with the California mess. One of those friends actually spent part of his youth here since his father was serving in the U.S. Air Force.

In my final chapter, I better explain finding a new friend in the San Antonio area. My local friend made a strong push for me to buy a dog similar to her Irish Jack Russell. I must admit that I took an immediate liking to the personality of that smaller breed. Throughout my life, I've had many dogs, most often sheepdogs such as Kelpies,, Blue Heelers, and Border Collies.

By mid-November 2019, I found a ranch 70 miles away that offered Irish Jack Russell pups for sale. When I found the right pup, I made a deposit and adopted this little gal during the next month. I expect that my life will change when I add the new puppy to my daily routine. I look forward to such a change.

I named this pup Red Molly for the reddish tint to the hair on her head. That is not the only time red shows up in my life. I try to spend quality time on my back porch. I have noticed two types of birds that come to visit me. The dozen or so sparrows are rather common and non-descript. The other visitors are a pair of red cardinals, formally named the Northern Cardinal. They are commonly found from Canada to Mexico, more so in the eastern portion of the country. In my case, I get to enjoy the bright red male who likes to chase away the smaller sparrows so he can get priority on the new bird feeder. As is the case in the bird community, the female partner has a more subdued color. The entire group of birds brings joy to my backyard.

As I finalized my decision, Bobbi chastised me for not consulting with her. She was probably right; however, with the many changes to my life, I assumed that it was my decision time, and I was the decision-maker. Even if I had consulted her, I am quite sure that the outcome would have been the same.

As I did my distant shopping, I was in the middle of my cancer battle and trying to finalize a divorce process. I started my cancer battle living on the remote ranch. Midway through this battle, my health took a nosedive, and I ended up spending eight days in a Reno hospital. I have to give my son, Christian, credit for being the first to realize that being home alone at a time like this was not a good idea. He came to rescue me and put me up in his house where I had my own bedroom. Soon after this step, I realized that I should put this ranch up for sale, so I had the freedom to pursue my new Plan-B.

During the cancer fight, I realized that this challenge had made me humble. Humble seems to be the right word as I felt destroyed physically and emotionally. Regarding the physical set back, I found a gym close to my home that should help with some of the recovery. The emotional recovery is happening over time.

My ability to travel to S.A. was based upon a favorable cancer prognosis from my Reno doctor, Dr. Singh. That did not come about until the first week in July 2019. As soon as the last PET scan indicated that my cancer was gone, I was in my pickup headed to Texas. I drove for four days stopping halfway to visit Bobbi in Nebraska.

So, during this one-year transition, a thought or motto came to mind, and that was, "Keep Calm and Chive On."

So, when people ask why S.A. I have to admit that it was a long shot and that part of the decision process was making a wild guess on the best destination.

So, the short answer will remain, "I am not sure how I ended up here." But as time passes, I believe that there was divine guidance. Somehow, stronger powers helped move me to this warm and inviting city.

This chapter continues to unfold as I clean up this draft. With time, it becomes more evident that San Antonio was a great choice for a whole lot of reasons. The reasons include the whole shebang: climate, a nice home, a great neighborhood, amenities close by, and a growing list of personal friends.

The Life and Death of Larry Burrows

Incident Date: 10 Feb 1971

Larry Burrows is depicted in the opposing page photo, which was taken approximately one hour after I met him and a few hours before he died.

On the morning of 10 February 1971, I was in the HMM-364 ready room preparing for a flight to Khe Sanh. This was an unusual mission to a less-traveled part of Vietnam. Khe Sanh was a hot spot years prior, but during my tour of duty, it was not part of our normal operating area. In the late 1960s, the Marine Corps Area of Operation had moved south closer to Da Nang. In previous years, Marine helicopters flew hundreds, perhaps thousands of missions in support of Marines stationed up north. One of the other frequently visited Marine bases was Quang Tri, located between Khe Sanh and the Gulf of Tonkin.

For perspective, my squadron mate, Pat Kenny, has shared some statistics on his Facebook page. It breaks down the military casualties of the four military sectors in Vietnam. I-Corps was the top sector closest to the DMZ. The Army wanted to call this 1-Corps, but the Marines wanted to put their own stamp on their sector and thus called it I (eye) Corps.

The total casualties for I-Corps were 26,111. If you add up all of the casualties for the other three Corps, it came to 23,048. These numbers make it plain to see where the action was. Laos had 728 casualties, and we weren't even supposed to be there. The combat photographer deaths were not counted in the above numbers.

As a sad side story, when my father would watch CBS News with Walter Cronkite, he would hear daily reports of Marine pilot casualties. Around 1968, Cronkite visited Vietnam to see the war first hand. He shocked many when he reported that we were not winning the war. With each new CBS casualty report, my father was convinced that one of them must certainly be his son. So, he would pull up a chair on the front porch and wait for the black sedan with the chaplain to drive up and break the news. My year-long tour must have chewed him up. I still feel heartache when sharing this personal story.

I was the co-pilot on this mission even though I had long been designated as Aircraft Commander. I believe that the pilot was Major Van Leeuwen as he was senior to me and had more experience. Our mission was to transport the Commanding General to a large U.S. Army command briefing held at the base at Khe Sanh. This command briefing was mainly for U.S. Army and South Vietnamese forces preparing to launch into Laos. Perhaps the Marine Commander wondered why Marine Forces were not included.

As a prelude to this story, the skies over Vietnam drew dark as hundreds of Army Hueys, the mainstay helo for the U.S. Army, flew north to prepare for this operation. On the other hand, the mainstay helo for the Marine Corps was the CH-46.

As our briefing started that morning, we were interrupted by the *Time-LIFE* combat photographer Larry Burrows. He sought a ride up north so he could do his job of combat reporting. He was well aware that Operation Lam Son 719 was underway, and he was attracted to combat like a moth to a flame. On that day, based upon the fact that our support mission was sensitive, perhaps classified, we were unable to transport any news personnel.

Normally, we could transport these individuals. When this was explained to Larry Burrows, he graciously understood and said he would find a ride through other means. Little did I know that a few hours later, he would be dead.

As it turned out, he and his team of four combat photographers traveled south of Marble Mountain Air Facility to a South Vietnamese base, where they found a Huey willing to transport them. This was the location of the Huey and Burrows sketch at the top of this story.

Our mission was routine as we picked up the General and traveled north. We dropped him off for his briefing. He told us to get airborne and avoid any trouble. He would contact us later for a pickup and return flight.

We had been airborne for some time when the local DASC control agency asked if we were available to do a VR (visual recon) of a reported crash site. We agreed and then flew west towards Laos. We were able to locate the burning wreckage. From our high overflight, we quickly realized that there were no survivors. The wreckage had already burned and no bodies, alive or dead were visible. We reported no survivors. At that time, this wreckage was anonymous, with no clue who was on board.

For some of the crews flying north, we had been pre-briefed that there was a heavy gun position belonging to the enemy in the vicinity of the crash site. It is not clear if the South Vietnamese Huey crew was aware. It appears that the Huey crew flew low level right over the gun location, which may explain why they were shot down. When we did our VR fly over, we were at a safe altitude.

We later picked up our General and returned to the Air Facility at Marble Mountain.

Later that evening, when listening to Armed Forces radio, we learned that Larry Burrows, Henri Huet, Kent Potter, the only American, and Keisaburo Shimamoto had been killed in a helo crash. It was soon clear that they were the victims in the crash site we flew over. Larry Burrows was a special correspondent as far as Marines were concerned. This respect started when he covered a Marine Helo crew from a squadron by the call sign of Yankee Papa 13. This coverage would have been around 1968. This was a 12-page photo essay published in LIFE magazine. In fact, this was the cover story where the crew chief is in distress as he leans against the body of a dead helo pilot that they had just picked up. The crew chief was James Farley. Burrows had received the Capa Award for this photo. This one photo told an entire story. This *Time-LIFE* story also included an emotional picture of the crew chief back at the squadron area following the flights return to base. He was sitting on a footlocker with his head covered, hiding the tears of the day's events.

The Burrows crash story was later covered in the book, *Lost Over Laos,* co-written by Richard Pyle and Horst Faas. The push for this story started with the son of Burrows trying to find closure with a visit to the crash site. Finding the crash site was not as easy as it sounds. *Lost Over Laos* indicated that someone/somewhere had recorded the coordinates of the crash site.

As a point of interest, the border between Laos and South Vietnam was not marked. You would have to judge your distance from other checkpoints, such as Khe Sanh. President Nixon liked to tell the story that we were not operating in Laos. When our helo did the overflight, we were quite certain that the crash occurred on the South Vietnamese side of the border. This book points out that the site was many miles on the Laos side.

The book also points out that when the team found the crash site, they started to dig for clues. This was unnerving as there was un-expended ordnance still in the wreckage. The team did find the lens of a camera that was later tracked to a camera shop close to where Burrows lived in London. This was further evidence that they had found the actual crash site.

My memory of Burrows was a man with dark-rimmed glasses and a number of cameras hanging from his neck. Normally, these camera frames were dark-colored. Given the fact that these tools of trade had been banging off each other for years, most of the dark color on the cameras had been worked off or chipped off. He was clearly a dedicated combat photographer as he was in his 4th year of combat reporting. For the rest of us, one year in combat was more than enough.

I am sorry that Larry Burrow had to die in this manner; however, I *felt lucky* to have met him, even though it was on the day of his death.

Spiritual Development

Let me start with this simple statement, going to the Community Church in Paradise Valley exposed me to a spiritual lesson that I could understand. Our cowboy pastor is not ordained, but he knows his bible, and he is very motivated to share the gospel. He enjoys teaching the bible. In short, he is a very good pastor.

My exposure to Pastor Jerry Harper started shortly after I moved to Paradise Valley in 2006. I knew from the beginning that Jerry was different with a simpler message that appealed to me. His credentials were based on his simple and sincere rancher style of delivery, not attributed to any time at a fancy seminary. Jerry is the gentleman seated on the hay wagon in the illustration at the top of this story.

He had just finished an outdoor funeral for a local WW-II hero by the name of Bob Thomas. Bob flew P-51 Mustangs, maybe the coolest fighter plane of all time, from Normandy all the way into Germany. Bob's flag-draped casket is in the back of the hay wagon. Bob was Hitler's worst enemy because he was a resolute fighter pilot determined to chase the Germans all the way back to Berlin. He was not only strong-willed, but he had a reputation for being a great pilot. At one point, the Germans shot down his P-51 Mustang, and he was back flying the next day.

What added to Pastor Jerry's spiritual appeal was the fact that this Godly message was absent all of the smoke and mirrors, without the emphasis on ceremony over substance.

Looking back, I have attended church since I was a little kid. My parents took me to the Manitou Lutheran church on a regular basis. I was too young to grasp what lessons were being taught each Sunday, but I was not too young to understand religion through the eyes of my Norwegian grandmother, Thea. She was from the old school and believed that neither joy nor pleasure could be found in a spiritual life. We were on this planet to suffer and be strict to the biblical teachings. For example, the following items were strictly prohibited: alcohol, smoking, card playing, dancing, etc. I was taught to lead my life with the constant question, "What would you like to be doing when Jesus comes?" It was a kind of fearful version of God's love.

Later my father softened the harsh message and assured me that God did not intend us to be without joy and pleasure. We could do some things in life without being subject to eternal damnation.

My religious commitment seemed minimal as I attended college and went to Naval Flight School.

Along the way, I was exposed to some lackluster military chaplains.

My quest for a spiritual connection did get stronger when I went to combat in Vietnam (1970-71). I became even more grateful for God's forgiveness when I got shot down and nearly killed. I did acknowledge that there may be a divine power that might be able to protect me.

When I got married in 1970, I was pushed into a Catholic indoctrination. This was odd because my then-wife, who pushed this, was a non-practicing Catholic girl. She criticized more church policies than she supported. This seemed odd to me. It also seemed odd to be exposed to the Catholic concept of guilt. Because I never really bought into the Catholic way of thinking, I searched for a compromise church.

This led to the Episcopal Church in Laguna Beach. The elder priest and the younger were both impressive. They were impressive as creative thinkers more than spiritual leaders. I don't remember any weekly bible lessons and teaching that would guide us through the next week. They did not seem very spiritual in the traditional sense. This church was also big on ceremony and the correct color robes during the various church holidays. I felt somewhat disconnected from organized religion. For all I knew, this was the way I thought things were supposed to be.

The only sermon that I remember was when we were asked to meditate on our hand. Think about the motions that it can perform with simple commands from our brain. This silly theme carried on for 15-20 minutes. I came away no wiser.

The worst part was that I did not feel any spiritual development as I started to get older.

During my second marriage, my wife was a Baptist of sorts but had no interest in attending any particular churches, yet she was content to tag along as I attended Episcopal churches. Still, there was no real spiritual development. She never really expressed her personal feelings about religion. It was all kind of mox nix.

During this marriage, my first son was born premature and almost died during his second week. I was about to witness my first Godly miracle. The hospital chaplain, a defrocked priest, asked if I wanted my son to be baptized. I said, sure, I will take care of this in good time. He looked me in the eye and said there might not be another chance because he is dying in front of our eyes. I quickly changed my mind, and the baptism was conducted inside the incubator. Within 30 seconds, nurses started to point out a number of monitors starting to move from scary readings to something approaching normal, i.e., lung oxygen processing, etc. Doctors rushed into the intensive care room with eyes wide open, asking each other, "What in the world is going on here?"

The salvation of saving my premature son was an example of a God Wink. A really big God Wink.

That miracle happened before my very eyes.

This could be written off as a sheer coincidence, but I did not believe this cynical theory. I believed that he turned the corner when the baptism ceremony took place. This made me a stronger believer and improved my faith in God. My mother was present and also shared the same impression.

Unfortunately, there was so much turmoil in this second marriage that I had little time to focus on religion.

Things settled down in my 3rd marriage. We attended church because we thought it was our spiritual obligation. This church, located at Lake Tahoe, had a loving and kind Episcopal priest. Unfortunately, he was quietly and quickly removed when he was accused of sexual misconduct with a female member of the congregation. This was rather unsettling. No one was privy to any details. He was there in good standing one day and gone the next.

I moved to Reno and started to attend a beautiful Episcopal Church near the Truckee River. Again, pomp and ceremony, but not much substance. I can barely remember anything more than a one-paragraph biblical reading per service. Sermons seemed focused on contemporary issues in the world, yet did not seem to offer spiritual lessons. I wasn't sure why I wasted this one-hour per week.

Despite the fact that I could not manage to finish either War and Peace or Anna Karenina, I did become a huge fan of the author Leo Tolstoy.

Tolstoy was never a religious man in his prime. I was able to read his shorter book, *Confessions*. As he aged, he was puzzled why people of religion generally seemed to be happier. This puzzle caused him to focus on or study various religions. After careful study, he concluded that basic religion was generally good, and the organized church had a very bad history.

I relate to this conclusion. I see so much hypocrisy in the rich and fancy church, especially those slick-haired evangelists. From the Middle Ages forward, the worst of the worst was the Catholic Church. The hypocrisy became even worse when that church started to attract male pedophiles. If the church had been honest with all of this, it would have tackled this problem head-on early on. Instead, they elected to cover it up by moving bad priests who offended again. Today, that church still reels from the harm that it caused hundreds if not thousands of victim families—all of this madness under the banner of God.

When you read the details of the Crusades into the Holy Land, the slaughter of women and children does not seem to match any church teaching, especially the lessons of Jesus.

Then I moved to Paradise Valley and met Pastor Jerry. I learned about God's grace and how it was an undeserved gift to us. Good deeds had nothing to do with salvation because otherwise, we would be able to brag that we did better things than our neighbors, and thus we must be better Christians.

Also, the previous idea about guilt was not a factor in Jerry's teachings.

We learned about church history in a context that related to our daily lives. We learned the difference between the harsh order of the Old Testament and the love of God in the New Testament. This is the contrast of the old covenant and the new covenant. This topic had to be taught.

I have been taught that the only sacrifice God demands of me is for me to be thankful and to praise him for his vast glory. The other key is to, "Believe in me." This is a rather easy assignment compared to what my Grandmother taught me.

It is easy to say that I have learned more in fourteen years from Pastor Jerry than I learned in my prior life span.

Now when Sunday comes around, I look forward to the weekly church service. I know that I am going to actually learn something. I am even happy to leave a San Francisco 49'er football game, so I can attend church.

As I settled into San Antonio, one of the challenges was to find a new church to replace the old cowboy church. This was not an easy task. I tried many churches and, for various reasons, had trouble finding a good fit. I ended up checking out a couple of Lutheran churches since that was the religion that I grew up in.

I did not find a church home until I stumbled into a late afternoon service in a small church vestry. This small setting was more comfortable and more closely resembled the small church setting that I left in Paradise Valley. I think this will be the church that I now call home.

My spiritual development actually took a lifetime. *I feel lucky* that my church experience in Paradise Valley seemed to open my eyes and open my heart. Once again, I was lucky to find true religion before my life was spent. Remember, the best sermons are lived, not preached.

Short Shorts

70+ Years worth of close call stories.

Drinking Gas: it did not taste that good

My first close call story came at a very early age. I was around five years old, living on the family farm. My mother had been painting a building and left out some small tomato cans with gasoline so she could clean paintbrushes.

Being a curious little guy, I apparently drank some of the gasoline and then passed out. Later, my mother happened by and found me unconscious and very purple. She panicked. Not knowing what to do with me, she decided to drag me to a field a half-mile away from where my father was cultivating with the tractor. She was not very gentle as my father described this event as an ugly sight. My mother was dragging me by the leg, bouncing my sick head off the ground.

When she finally arrived at my father's location, he was cool-headed as he immediately stuck his finger down my throat to make me hurl up the poison. After that, he had to give me a couple of emergency breaths. Within a couple of minutes, I started to breathe again, and my color started to return.

My father likes to tell the story that if the gasoline did not kill me, the half-mile drag should have.

Eating a Clothesline at High Speed: that did not taste good either

I had a traumatic event during the middle of high school. I had finished basketball practice, and I needed to find my dad for a ride home. As I stepped out of the school building, I noticed that he was driving away. At this point, the conditions outside were pitch dark.

I thought I needed to run him down, or he would leave me. I did a high-speed sprint across the schoolyard, trying to get an angle on his car. I was running as fast as I possibly could. My progress was abruptly halted as I hit a close line wire, eye level. This impact put me upside down, landing on the back of my head.

I think he heard the impact and my cry out in pain. The clothesline wire ripped open both eyes to the point that I could no longer see.

I crawled into the back seat of the car as he drove me home. By this time, I was bleeding heavily from my face, and especially from both eyes wounds. By the time we got home, blood had pooled on the back seat of the car, and yet my father had no idea about the face damage.

When he helped me out of the car, he realized that he needed to turn around and take me back to the Stanley hospital, where they stitched up cut wounds on both eyes.

I was a big hit the next day at school because both eyes were purple, and the stitch scars were very obvious. I guess I looked like a wounded, tough guy. I also wondered why my teachers kept staring at me.

Motorcycle Crash:

After college, I competed in cross-country motorcycle events. These were long-distance endurance races with breakneck speed over unknown terrain. Many of these events included my good friend, Steve Hyde. Midway through a daylong race, I was headed up a steep hill at around 40 to 45 mph. As I came over the top, my motorcycle went airborne.

Unfortunately, my most likely landing spot was filled by a very large boulder, around 3 feet tall. I knew if I impacted this rock, it would be a hard crash. I tried to change my direction and angle in midair. When I did hit the ground next to the boulder, my bike was sideways. I put out my left leg to break the fall.

When I landed, my knee snapped and twisted. The motorcycle and I crashed and rolled over many times.

I was not able to finish the race, so Steve helped me limp my bent-up motorcycle back to the starting line. It was a long and painful journey to retrace our miles.

This is the knee that required corrective surgery a couple of years later.

Car Crash at Lake Tahoe:

While the family was living at Lake Tahoe, I took the two dogs for a run on the east shore of the lake. It was Memorial Day, and many fools were drinking and driving.

By late afternoon, I returned my dogs to the old Land Cruiser, and we started to pull unto the main road to return home. By the time I had my road speed up to around 45 mph, I heard screeching tires around the corner in front of me. About two seconds later, I saw a muscle car coming at me sideways, taking up most of the two lanes of travel.

My only choice was to eat the guardrail on my right, which trapped me into my lane. The car coming at me was doing around 85 mph, and it clipped the front left portion of my car.

The impact was so hard that one of my dogs, Tedi, was rocketed out the rear window. Also, the impact blew out the drive shaft of the Land Cruiser to 20' behind the accident scene. I had my seat belt on, but the car was too old for airbags.

The ambulance wanted to treat me and then transport me to a hospital. I felt that I had no choice but to refuse medical service so I could search for my missing Blue Heeler. That task seemed to be the top priority. Unfortunately, though I called her and searched as well as I could, it seemed Tedi was long gone.

While waiting for the highway patrol to arrive, I went over to the location of the other drivers. It turns out the two drivers had been at a beach party. I asked who the driver that hit me was, and the fellow I suspected pointed in both directions. One of his buddies replied by calling him an ass hole. Needless to say, that this punk kid, around 18 or 19, was in handcuffs about two minutes after NHP arrived.

I had my head imprint into the door frame. My left shoulder suffered most of the impact. I still feel the effects of that injury today as I type this story. I discovered in a subsequent MRI was that the accident also broke seven vertebrae broken. The only good news is that the accident cash settlement came to around $59K. Later this settlement money was used to purchase my new ranch land in Paradise Valley. We used that money to pay for the ranch property, so this was not all bad.

The other good news is that almost three months after the accident, I received a call from someone who lived in a nearby town. He'd found a dog and called to see if she was mine. It is always a great event when you get reconnected with a lost pet.

I guess *I was lucky on a couple of fronts here.*

Another Motorcycle Crash in the Philippines:

While stationed in the Philippines, I rented a cabaña in upper Subic Bay. I chose this location, so while I was trying to save my marriage, my first wife could come out so we could spend some time together.

In order to commute to the base where the carrier was docked, I had to find transportation, and. I ended up buying a used 250cc Honda. It was old but seemed to serve me well.

One day, I must have been behind schedule because I was driving faster than normal. I came to a left-hand curve on a very rough road. If you have ever lived in the Philippines, you know that all roads are rough. Potholes are the norm. While in the curve, one of the potholes washed out the back end of the bike, and I went down into a slide.

As I hit the pavement, I was sliding and looking back over my shoulder. I realized that a sugar cane truck was about to run over my ass. It was only about 15 yards behind me. With clever navigation, I was able to drag one elbow and one heel so that I was sliding off the road instead of down the road. I am pretty sure this was a typical Philippine truck with no brakes. I managed to slide to the edge of the road as the truck roared by.

And so, goes another day *getting lucky and staying lucky.*

Reunion

It all started with a passing comment from my sister Kathy and her brother-in-law Wiggy about a year prior, "Why don't we try to get all Riersgard family members for a reunion sometime?"

Kathy set a date for 10-12 July 2015. She was gracious enough to be the host for a large group. We knew going in that we were going to have a good turnout. We only had three missing family members. Lauren was tied up with her new job in San Diego and could not break away. Raymie was also tied up, and Drew could not attend. Everyone else was present. Raymie is Carol's daughter. Drew (Andrew) is Marsha's son.

I made the commitment early. My challenge was to find someone to sit the ranch for a week, and eventually, I did find a fellow to help for a week. This would allow me to make the drive in our new Mini Cooper.

Early planning called for Christian (CFR) and Liza to join us. Four people in the car would save some money and provide ample spare drivers. Because CFR just enrolled in a high tempo school program at Truckee Meadows Community College, he was not sure he could skip school to attend. Over time, he got brave and decided to skip school briefly.

My sisters and I agreed that we would save homestead profit money to help cover the costs of kids flying in or driving in. This allowed the full purchase price for Steffen's family and Christian's family. I paid for their rental car, and I covered the food cost contribution to Kathy. As a result, these cash strapped campers could attend at little or no money.

I planned for a 2.5-day drive until Kathy put on pressure for me to arrive early. She wanted an immediate family in early so we could visit before the crowd got too big and wild. I drove for 12 hours a day for two days to make that schedule.

The plan was for family members to stumble in on Thursday. My boys could not arrive until Friday. We anticipated Cousin Phil and sisters to arrive sometime Thursday. They did not arrive until late in the day, and thus the anticipation was high as we wondered when we would see the long-lost cousins.

I am not sure how to describe the first meeting, as it had been 60 years since I saw them. I guess we had a short visit to Moscow, ID during that period, but my memory does not register many details.

I did recognize Phil, and this was my first meeting with his wife, Char. I did not recognize either Linda or Marsha. Phil looked similar to his dad. Linda was smaller than I had imagined. Actually, her stature resembles her mother, Olive. Marsha was the tallest of all these cousins.

That first night we started storytelling. Phil was up to bat first. He recounted his long and interesting work life that included many stops around the globe. Some of this work was associated with the Peace Corps. My turn was the next night. We got Linda to contribute with some help from family member questions. She, too, was a world traveler, but that was to be expected as she was an FSO (Field Services Officer) for the State Department. Marsha had similar tales, but she remained closer to home, to be closer to her aging parents.

Over time some of the 4th generation kids told their stories; however, some escaped before they could talk. The kids that did tell stories helped fill in many gaps that were missing over the past 60 years.

While at Kathy's so-called cabin, we mingled, we drank wine, and we ate well. On Saturday, the group ended up at Grandpa Christ's homestead site. That event started with the land renter, Kevin, providing a farm overview of his scheme for land management. He shared many new progressive farming techniques that would have been unthinkable one generation ago, for example, don't cultivate wheat straw into the soil).

Next, I provided a historical overview of Grandpa Christ's homestead. This talk was based upon his early years living on the homestead. It seems strange that I told a story that was 60 years past. At that time, the homestead was fully functional with all of the structures standing. Farm life was still unfolding; however, Grandpa Christ only had six more years before his death in 1958. This oral presentation was a close parallel to the homestead perspective written by Uncle Ken. The sketch at the bottom of this story illustrates what the original homestead looked like.

On Sunday, the day after the tour, folks started to pack up and head home.

I set a more comfortable driving pace. I drove to Billings the first afternoon. I made it to Jackpot, NV the next night, and I was home by noon the following day. It was time to relieve the ranch sitter.

The event was a great success. We agreed to do this event again in the future. We did not tackle the operative question of what we should do with the original homestead ownership. Currently, the ownership is like a pie that has been cut into many pieces.

It turned out to be a very nice family, after all. Many of us had been split apart for long periods of time, and now we were getting reacquainted. What is more, everyone in this gathering was getting along beautifully.

Since the first reunion, Cousin Linda and I went to work on the Riersgard family history. There were certain skills that I brought to the table and some different skills that Linda brought to the table. She discovered that interesting personal detail was often only available through church records.

At this point, the new family tree was front and center. This topic has already been covered in a previous chapter.

While Linda and I toiled, I received a message from a fellow named Dennis Reiersgard. He made a simple declaration that we shared the same grandfather. This story has also been shared earlier in this book.

There will be a shared session of family history at the next reunion, but Dennis gets to kick off that program with his story. In short, Christ Reiersgard fathered a son by the name of Milton and apparently never knew it.

The major change from the first reunion to the next reunion will be the introduction of more grandchildren, as well as the introduction of our new-found cousin, Dennis.

I feel a *lot of luck* being associated with this family and all of its moving parts, past present, and future.

Final Chapter

When I started this writing project, I had a simple image of my life span, which seemed to arc over four chapters.

- First my youth, from farm boy through college
- Second my 20 years in the Marine Corps
- Third my law enforcement career
- Fourth my 14 years on a remote ranch

Not realizing that I could live this long, it now appears that there may be a fifth chapter unfolding in front of me. This would include my time after the ranch as I transition to South Texas. Time will tell how long this chapter will last but one thing for certain, this is the final chapter.

This chapter starts with plenty of uncertainty. As I left the ranch, I am dealing with my cancer, licking my wounds from a divorce, and looking forward to an unknown future. While part of this is exciting, there is still the stress of dealing with the hand that life just dealt me.

As soon as my Reno cancer doctor informed me that I was rid of my cancer, I jumped into my pickup truck and headed south. I knew that I was ready for a warmer climate and a radical change to my life. Yet, I was still uncertain where I would end up. I had considered other locations but soon eliminated a few of them. Along the way, I asked advice from friends familiar with some spots I was considering.

On the long meandering drive from Reno to Texas, I stopped to visit a dear old friend. She and I had a long history dating back to college. Our friendship in college blossomed into an on-again and off-again romantic relationship in the years that followed. Those encounters had to be carefully planned around other relationships and marriages along the way. While there was a lot of substance in our relationship, we never managed to get past the category of best friends. This was true for over 50 years. I've never come close to this kind of relationship with anyone else.

While I was anxious to arrive in Texas, I was also content to spend some quality time visiting her outside of Seward, Nebraska. As this visit unfolded, I had the luxury of good home cooking and good company. I was able to get some support and healing as we talked endlessly. We talked about the past, the present, and even ventured into the future.

The future was the complicated part. Neither of us knew what the future might have in store. After two days, we hugged, kissed, and I was on my way. This last sentence may summarize our relationship over the previous five decades. We would find each other, rekindle our relationship, discuss the future, and I would leave. This pattern has taken its toll as my friend was also losing trust in me. I had a habit of driving off, again and again.

During the early stages of this chapter, this lady friend wanted to remain anonymous, but later she agreed that I could add a name to this segment. Her name is Bobbi, and she is very special.

As it turned out, I settled in San Antonio. When I arrived in San Antonio, new friends and acquaintances asked me why I picked this city. I could not seem to find a logical answer. I couldn't decide if the divine influence was at play here or it was a complete accident. But honestly, I think God must have moved me in that direction without me realizing it.

The stark reality of arriving in a new city of two million people was that I did not know anyone. No family and no friends were nearby. The good news was that this was a friendly city that actually felt more like a large town than a city.

Soon after my arrival, my youngest sister contacted me and informed me that one of her very best friends lived in the nearby community of Boerne. Her name was Jane. I knew of her from family connections in Stanley, North Dakota. We both grew up in the same small town. As mentioned in the chapter titled *Reflections*, she spent a lot of time at my father's house, where she sometimes took shelter from her family dynamics. Later, Jane would write a heartfelt thank you letter to my father for the role he played in her formative years. This letter arrived at a very opportune time because my dad was dying of cancer, and that letter meant a great deal. As best we can determine, that original letter managed to get lost along the way.

On the home front, I promptly found a beautiful Mediterranean style home that I purchased. It was the right size. It was upscale, and it was in a very nice suburban neighborhood. It cost more than I had anticipated; however, my finances were sound thanks to the family oil revenue. In short, I could afford this nice new home.

As I settled into my new home, I started to visit Jane 30 miles down the road. She took me under her wing and included me in her well-established social circles. This included both her friends and her family nearby. We would generally spend time socializing on the weekends. This included dinners, dances, movies, and regional travel. It was not long before our photos showed up on Facebook, and the first lady friend started to wonder about the second lady friend.

Jane has a reputation as a wild child or party girl. In our short time together, she has lived up to this reputation. This was especially true as we traveled to Fredericksburg for a casual day together. While I visited the National Museum of the Pacific War, Jane ventured down the street to a piano bar. Later, after I departed the museum, I called her to ask about her location. She could not tell me because she was mildly shit faced. The bartender finally got on the phone to give me directions. When I arrived, Jane was moving from table to table, making friends. She had the whole bar in an uproar. She was also making friends with the piano player just to make sure that the party atmosphere did not abate. This was a fun time as I got to see her in her relaxed mode. Yes, Jane was now living up to her reputation, and it was a scene to remember.

While the two relationships were well defined and different, they may not have looked different. One was an old romance that had cooled off, and the other was what Jane called Best Buddies. There was a lot of quality time together, but no romance. At one point, the lady friend I'd known longest confronted me about my new lady friend, and I was able to honestly explain myself. In short, I never expected to have this dilemma at this stage of my life. Oh, to have two good looking blondes in my life; the final chapter of my life was getting interesting. How lucky can I get, to have this situation at this age?

Moving on from the topic of female relationships, I continued to settle into my new home town. I had to find essential services ranging from church, grocery store, bank, post office, gym, a suitable park to walk in, good restaurants, and so on. This search also included my return to the local VA system. Old age was taking its toll on my body, and the VA was determined to patch me up and take care of my medical needs.

In addition to getting used to my new home, I also needed to adjust to my new daily routine. I no longer needed to get up early, feed the sheep, and strike out on countless ranch projects and chores. Now, I needed to get used to quality time at home, quiet time where I could sit on the back porch and enjoy the dog or read. As mentioned, I had time for long leisurely walks in the park. This turned out to be one of my favorite times in the day.

In order to travel to these many locations mentioned above, I needed a choice of transportation. I could continue to drive my large pickup truck with 15 mpg, or I could find an alternative. My alternative ended up being a new 300 cc Vespa scooter. The Texas weather was ideal for a scooter, and it was fun to ride. My home is in the north suburbs, and the roads are ideal for scooter travel. This became even more interesting as I found a front dog carrier so I could transport my new dog to the nearby park for our daily walk. The soft carrier allows her to stick her head out if she wants some wind in her face, or she can duck inside for cover. My dog, Red Molly, is still young and only around 8 pounds, so she is the right size for this kind of transportation.

Red Molly is an Irish Jack Russell. I came upon this dog idea when I visited Jane in Boerne. She had an adult dog that is the same breed. Her dog and I took a liking to each other, so it was not long before I was online searching for a suitable pup from the same breed.

When I packed up the ranch, about one-third of my belongings were destined for Texas. I sent a lot of stuff to Goodwill, and the rest was left behind as part of the ranch purchase. Since I had no good idea where I was headed, I was uncertain what to pack and what to leave behind. For some reason, I packed up my favorite dog leash. I must have known that there might be a dog in my future.

Back to Bobbi from Nebraska, she called to announce that she was jealous. First, she was jealous of my friendship with Jane. Second, she was jealous of the mild Texas weather as she was enduring another cold winter. Finally, she was jealous that I was going out every weekend for fun times. She explained that she was now stressed out, and she wanted to spend more time together traveling. As we started to make early plans for travel during the summer of 2020, the coronavirus fell upon us. It fell hard, and it fell fast, especially for my age group and even more so for people with underlying conditions, as is my case. At the time of this writing, the plan is to travel as little as possible and to avoid crowds. So, spending more time together has been put on hold.

Cancer was mentioned at the top of this story. It was also briefly mentioned earlier in this book. At the time of publishing, the cancer story is not quite over yet. In May of 2020, the lymphoma cancer came back. That seems to be one of two basic rules for lymphoma. First, this type of cancer is treatable, and second, it tends to come back. My cancer return was faster than normal because it was back within nine months of being cancer clean.

My first cancer battle was in Reno. I was under the care of the very talented Dr. Singh. It was not until he cleared me to travel that I actually made my move to Texas. Now that I am in Texas, I started my cancer care through the local VA hospital. The VA tries very hard to provide top-notch care, but their resources are limited, and that eventually affects cancer care. After it became apparent that the cancer was coming back, I made the decision to get a second opinion from MD Anderson. Their closest large medical campus is in Houston. Again, I seem to have found a talented cancer doctor. The drive to Houston takes three-and-one-half hours, but this is an investment in my future.

All this means is that I need to prepare for another treatment battle. I managed to survive the previous six-month treatment battle, and therefore, I can do it again. My nearby friend in Boerne has indicated that she will care for me and support me if the treatment becomes unusually tough. With all of this said, I am in a good frame of mind and ready for whatever comes my way.

When asked how I feel, my answer is consistently positive. I feel good. The problem with cancer is that it is an insidious disease. I can feel good on the outside while the cancer is starting its destruction on the inside.

As another plus here, my oldest son and his family plan to move to San Antonio during the summer of 2020. This will provide the luxury of family support if I need family help during the upcoming treatment routine. My son, Christian, was very helpful during the tough times of the first treatment, and he is prepared to help again when he arrives.

Who knows how many years remain under this chapter. I will update this until my draft goes to self-publishing. But this is definitely the final chapter.